# european ideologies since 1789:
## rebels, radicals and political ferment

# european ideologies since 1789:
## rebels, radicals and political ferment

**edited by**    **thomas e. hachey**
**and**
**ralph e. weber**

marquette university

ROBERT E. KRIEGER PUBLISHING COMPANY
HUNTINGTON, NEW YORK
1981

Original Edition 1981
(*Some material originally published under the title, "Voices of Revolution"*)

Printed and Published by
ROBERT E. KRIEGER PUBLISHING COMPANY, INC.
645 NEW YORK AVENUE
HUNTINGTON, NEW YORK 11743

Copyright © 1972 (original book and contents) by
THE DRYDEN PRESS, INC.
Transferred to
Thomas Hachey & Ralph Weber, March 1, 1979
Reprinted by Arrangement

Printed in the United States of America

Library of Congress Cataloging in Publication Data

Hachey, Thomas E.
    European ideologies since 1789.

    Reprint of part 1 of Voices of Revolution published by the Dryden Press, Hinsdale, Ill.
    1. Revolutions—Europe—Addresses, essays, lectures.
2. Revolutionists—Europe—Addresses, essays, lectures.
I. Weber, Ralph Edward, joint author.    II. Title.
[HM283.H3  1980]        303.6'4'0922        80-12562
ISBN 0-89874-082-7

For Susan E. Siefert and Joseph F. Marcey, Jr.

# preface

So often in historical accounts, great revolutionary leaders and writers appear without their works and rhetoric. Rather, these men and occasional women are briefly described in their historical setting, and a perfunctory summary is given of their contribution. Aware of this, we have sought out the ideas, speeches, and writings of the major world revolutionaries over the last two hundred years. The selections which follow contain their evaluation of society and their visions of the world which should be. Many of the selections also reveal the deep anger and frustration which these revolutionaries experienced.

Those interested in the course of revolution, those curious about the rhetorical approach to major protest, those in the disciplines of history, political science, sociology, and English may find in this book the outstanding figures whose ideas, ideals, and visions helped to change a ruler, or a society, or a civilization, or, finally, the world.

The vagaries of spelling and punctuation have been retained for the most part in order to preserve the style of the era or original manuscript. Obvious spelling errors in the original have been corrected.

THOMAS E. HACHEY
RALPH E. WEBER

Marquette University
Milwaukee, Wisconsin
January 1980

# contents

Preface / vii
Introduction / 1

Maximilien Robespierre / 9
Louis Kossuth / 21
Giuseppe Mazzini / 31
Giuseppe Garibaldi / 43
Pierre Proudhon / 55
Mikhail Bakunin / 65
Karl Marx / 79
Leo Tolstoy / 91
William Morris / 109
Peter Kropotkin / 119
Georges Sorel / 131
Emmeline Pankhurst / 145
Lenin / 157
James Connolly / 173
Leon Trotsky / 183

# introduction

*If a man does not keep pace with his companions, perhaps it is because he hears a different drummer. Let him step to the music which he hears, however measured or far away.*

Henry David Thoreau

Revolution is the narcotic of modern history. Under its compelling and hypnotic spell, men have altered destiny and entire nations have experienced delirious convulsions in transcending the spirit of their times. Frequently, revolution has left a people socially disoriented, emotionally traumatized, psychologically scarred, and spiritually disillusioned. Occasionally, it has liberated them psychically, physically, and politically.

It is difficult to distinguish illusion from reality in the revolutionary experience. Inspirational slogans often have generated myths which bear slight resemblance to the facts of history. "United we stand, divided we fall," "liberty, equality, and fraternity," "the proletarians have nothing to lose but their chains. They have a world to win. Working men of all countries, unite!" and "all power to the people," are a few of the watchwords which have mesmerized the multitudes. For some, the promise of the revolution became the reality, or at least partially so; for others, the dream became a nightmare.

Facile definitions of revolution have sometimes obscured the truth with idle generalizations and romantic incantations. "Revolutions are the festivals of the oppressed," or "revolutions are the locomotives of history," are two such examples from the literature of rebellion. Indeed, revolutions have toppled autocracies, broken the chains of tyranny, liberated the working classes, and more. But the American Protestant who rejoiced upon reading the Declaration of Independence may have wondered where the revolution was going when the United States made a treaty of alliance with Catholic France. Frenchmen who gleefully applauded the beheading of King Louis XVI, who for many symbolized the oppression of the *ancien régime*, probably reflected ruefully on the wisdom of their ecstasy during the frightening days of the "Reign of Terror." Russians who were enchanted by promises of "all land to the peasants" and "all factories for the workers" perhaps judged the privations of the past preferable to the forced regimentation and collectivization of Soviet life. Revolutions seldom, if ever, provide panaceas, and new grievances are sometimes substituted for old ones. The lesson of history is that revolutionary change has had both positive and negative features; that the radicalism of the revolutionary leadership opposed to the state frequently becomes reactionary when those leaders themselves control the state.

That the most crucial revolutionary processes are essentially political in nature is evidenced by the fact that their beginnings and their ends are themselves characteristically political: revolution begins with a political crisis and ends with a political settlement. Revolution is one of those emotion charged words which we invariably associate with "insurrection," "uprising," "rebellion," or "civil war." Almost always the word connotes violence or the use of armed force. And, indeed, most of the great revolutions of the past two centuries, the American, French, Russian, Chinese, and Cuban Revolutions, have been accompanied by much bloodshed. Yet the use of force or the resort to violence is not indigenous to revolutions in either political theory or in historic fact. A revolution may involve action in defiance of the law and yet be conducted without violence on the part of participants, as in the instance of the rebellion which Gandhi led in India by the method of civil disobedience.

All revolutions do have one common denominator: protest against prevailing authority. This authority may be the state, church, an economic system such as capitalism, a social institution such as the family, or an individual king, president, or dictator. Moreover, all revolutions introduce a fever, often called freedom, into the political affairs of empires, nations, or states; or into the social, cultural, or economic institutions of a given society, which may range from public morals or mores to racial rebellion, or from educational innovation to prison reform. Indeed, revolutions may serve as catalysts of change within the system or, alternately, may seek the complete overthrow of the system for reasons which may pertain to race, nationality, religion, economic status, or sex.

Revolutions can and do vary quite considerably in their nature and purpose. Romantic nationalism and middle class revolutions between 1789 and 1900 have been succeeded by ideological and proletarian revolutions in the twentieth century. In the former, the slogans and rhetoric reflected egalitarian objectives which in practice were seldom fulfilled after the middle class had achieved its own ends. In the latter, the orientation has been toward either a completely "classless" society, or one in which the working class predominates. While political revolutions have frequently sought the reform of existing socio-economic, cultural, or religious institutions, their primary objective has been the redistribution of political power.

An objective which is therefore sought in every revolution is change from the *status quo,* although the manner of such change will differ according to the period. Revolutions in an earlier age were usually preceded by demands for the overthrow of oppressive monarchs, or for the national unification of a race or people. The twentieth century is the first to speak of "the revolution of rising expectations," or of a "war on poverty." The revolutionary protest against authority extends even to the dictionary itself.

Over two hundred years ago, the American Revolution officially began with the Declaration of Independence. The most important characteristics of that Revolution included the idea that "consent of the governed" was crucial to good government. It should be noted that consent was not sought from women, Indians, slaves, and many unpropertied persons. Thus the reality of consent differed from the theory. The Revolution did, however, bring into practice some of the principles developed by John Locke and other early eighteenth century philosophers: that men have inalienable rights such as life, liberty, and the pursuit of happiness.

When American revolutionaries spoke of liberty, they meant it in political terms and did not, with one or two exceptions, apply it to the institution of slavery. In addition, the American Revolution did nothing to change the institution of private property. As the Revolution led to the Constitution, states retained the power over suffrage; too often that right extended only to those with property. Therefore, seen in the perspective of the last 200 years, the American Revolution, radical and daring for its time, was extremely moderate in both its aims and in its execution.

Revolution took a different turn in 1789. The French Revolution, like the American, was inspired by the tenets of the Enlightenment: rationalism, deism, and the idea of progress. But it was markedly different in its ideological tone. Both revolutions included internecine civil wars. In the American experience, however, monarchism versus republicanism was the central issue between loyalists and patriots, and opposing sides were not determined along strict socio-economic lines. By contrast, the French Revolution aligned the peasantry, the proletariat, and the bourgeoisie against the aristocracy. Moreover, the atrocities and terror of the French experience were much more intense than the American, fundamentally because it was a vicious class war in addition to being a political struggle.

Nineteenth century European revolutions were largely the product of continued class struggle and the growth of cultural and political nationalism. Some of the rebellions of the 1830's and 1840's derived from efforts to enfranchise a larger part of the bourgeois class; other revolutions of that century proceeded from the campaigns for national unification. It was during this period that Germany and Italy overcame their more stubborn disunity and emerged as nation-states. Formerly in the West, there had always been narrower allegiances—to municipality, guild, feudal lord, or the like—to compete with and divide the national loyalty of the individual. And there had also been wider allegiances—to the Holy Roman Empire, to a universal church, to the solidarity of an international aristocracy. By the third quarter of the nineteenth century, these older political loyalties were either dead or in decay. Nationalism became a religion for men like Louis Kossuth, Giuseppe Garibaldi, and Apolinario Mabini, and salvation for them took the form of revolution and the liberation of their homelands.

In many respects, industrialization had a greater influence in shaping the modern world than either the Enlightenment or the political revolutions. Industrialization depersonalized and, in some instances, dehumanized man. He lost his identity and his independence in the factory. The exploitation and abuses of capitalism gave rise to a reaction: socialism. In contradistinction to the bourgeois or nationalist revolutionaries of an earlier period, the socialist revolutionaries supported the rule of the working classes and control over the means and modes of production. Their expressed aim was not the abolition of private property, but rather the equitable distribution of it. Moderate socialists like William Morris, Pierre Proudhon, and Eugene V. Debs, anarchists like Mikhail Bakunin and Emma Goldman, and militant socialists like Karl Marx and Mao Tse-tung, each had his or her view of how this goal might best be achieved.

Although the first major revolution of the twentieth century erupted in Russia, subsequent revolutions have taken place in non-European worlds. Latin America, Asia, and Africa have been the scenes of violent protest against economic and/or political imperialism. These contemporary heartlands of revolution are seething with all of the volatile ingredients of emergent nationalism which once convulsed Europe; and they are being simultaneously subjected to the more recent revolutionary phenomenon of socialism.

A characteristic common to European, American, and Third World revolutionaries has been their determination either to free the oppressed or to secure the rights of minorities. Twentieth century proletarian and socialist revolutions were not the first to be concerned with the rights of women, or with those of minorities. But they did champion these causes more zealously than earlier revolutionaries, and often extended their appeal beyond the working classes to the poor and nonwhite races of the world. Final judgment on the achievements and consequences of these peculiarly different revolutionary experiences must await the further passage of time.

Revolutions too often have involved only surface changes, such as the transfer of power from one personality to another, or the replacement of one form of tyranny by another. But a vital or genuine revolution must be concerned with the triumph of human values and human rights. While there may be no common agreement on the means of achieving these ends among the revolutionaries included in this volume, all of them spoke and wrote about the essential needs of man and were exceedingly sensitive to the inequities surrounding them. Truly they marched to a "different drummer."

maximilien robespierre
louis kossuth
giuseppe mazzini
giuseppe garibaldi
pierre proudhon
mikhail bakunin
karl marx
leo tolstoy
william morris
peter kropotkin
georges sorel
emmeline pankhurst
lenin
james connolly
leon trotsky

# maximilien robespierre

Robespierre, a key figure during the period of the French Revolution and a leading member of both the Jacobin Club and the Committee of Public Safety, is most frequently associated with the "Reign of Terror" (1793-94) in France. Born at Arras on May 6, 1758, he was descended from a modest bourgeois family. His mother died when he was four years of age and shortly thereafter his father, an advocate who had gone bankrupt, deserted the family. Raised by grandparents, Robespierre attended a school conducted by the Oratorian order in Arras and later earned a scholarship to the College of Louis-le-Grand in Paris. A brilliant student, he matriculated in 1780, took a master's degree in law in 1781, and registered as an advocate at the Arras bar. He won admiration for his abilities, but his austerity and dedication isolated him from close companionships with either sex. Robespierre rapidly established a respected legal reputation and was appointed a judge in the Salle Épiscopale, a court with jurisdiction over the provostship of the diocese.

In the period following his return to Arras, Robespierre came under the influence of Rousseau's theories of democracy and deism. Already known as the advocate of the poor, he chastised the privileged classes, inveighed against royal absolutism, and decried arbitrary justice. Elected to the States-General of 1789, he labored for a time in obscurity but his influence in the Jacobin Club grew steadily and he soon became its president. Upon election to the Constituent

Assembly, Robespierre unsucessfully championed democratic elections and successfully backed a law which made members of the Constituent Assembly ineligible to the Legislative Assembly. Despite a weak voice and frail appearance (he was a slight man who stood only 5 feet 3 inches tall), Robespierre's biting rhetoric made him a forceful spokesman for his cause. He fought tenaciously for universal suffrage, for unrestricted entry to public offices and commissions, and for the right to petition. He opposed the veto, religious and racial discrimination and also defended actors, Jews, and blacks.

During the first two years of the French Revolution, Robespierre remained adamantly opposed to spreading revolution beyond the borders of France. He denounced the secret intrigues of the Court and of the royalists, their collusion with Austria, and the unpreparedness of the army. He violently attacked the marquis de Lafayette, the commander of the French Army, whom he suspected of wanting to establish a military dictatorship, but failed to obtain his dismissal and arrest. France's declaration of war against Austria and Prussia in April 1792 resulted in prompt military reverses for the French. A civil insurrection resulted which led to the formation of a new French assembly, the National Convention.

From the inception of the Convention in the latter part of September 1792, Robespierre, who was an elected representative of the Insurrectional Commune of Paris, condemned the majority Girondists for their inept direction of the war; the Girondists in turn accused Robespierre of seeking a personal dictatorship. The trial of King Louis XVI, which opened in December, heightened the conflict. Robespierre intervened eleven times during the course of the debates and his speech of December 3 (excerpts from this address follow) succeeded in rallying those who had been hesitant to kill the King.

But the execution of the King on January 21, 1793, did not resolve the struggle between the Girondins and the Jacobins; it only heightened passions on both sides. The treason of Girondist General Charles Dumouriez, who defected to the Austrian side in April, gave Robespierre the needed leverage to have the Convention suppress other Girondists during May and June, 1793. He was elected to a second Committee of Public Safety in July where his powers and prestige grew. The dangers of foreign invasion and the urgent need to maintain order and unity led the committee to inaugurate the "Reign of Terror." Although this was a collective effort, Robespierre's name is always most prominently associated with it. In order to clothe executive decrees with legitimacy, Robespierre, in what was also a tribute to the heroism of the soldiers in the French Army, asked the Convention in October 1793 to proclaim the Government of the Republic as the bona fide revolutionary government until peace was restored (excerpts from this speech follow).

Robespierre opposed both the extreme left, under Hébert, and the moderates led by Danton and Desmoulins, as evidenced by his address to the Convention on February 5, 1794 (excerpts from this speech also follow). The latter two had once been Robespierre's close comrades and it was with considerable reluctance that he ultimately supported their convictions and executions. Now faced by divisions within the Committee of Public Safety and no longer commanding the support of the independents who were a majority in the Convention, Robespierre found his position precarious. Perhaps most serious was the fact that he began to lose the support of the French people generally, whose hardships continued despite the recent French victories. It was precisely because the external threat from France's enemies no longer seemed as perilous that French people began to question the continued need for repressive measures at home.

Robespierre's motives and character have long been the subject of much debate. Some have considered him a ruthless dictator; others have judged him an idealistic champion of social revolution. It is now generally recognized that he did not make the Terror an instrument of personal ambition. To him, it was an expedient which was required for ruling in extraordinary circumstances. His courage, integrity, and devoted republicanism would seem to be above reproach.

Robespierre's address delivered before the Convention of July 26, 1794, was interpreted as presaging further purges and, on the following day, the forces of the right joined the independents in a dramatic rising which resulted in the arrest of Robespierre, his brother Augustin, and three close friends. On July 28, the Convention declared Robespierre to be an outlaw and ordered his execution. He was guillotined on the same evening on the Place de la Revolution (now the Place de la Concorde). Revolution was beginning to give way to reaction; and it had begun to devour its own children.

## Asking the Death Penalty For Louis XVI

CITIZENS! Without its knowledge, the Constituent Assembly has been turned aside from its proper task. The point is not merely that of trying the King. Louis is not the accused. You are not the judges! You are—you cannot be other than statesmen, the representatives of the nation. You have not to give a judgment for

From "Speeches of Maximilien Robespierre," as reprinted in *Voices of Revolt*, International Publishers, New York, 1927, I, 46-47, 51. The trial of the King was opened by the Constituent Assembly (the Convention). In December 3, 1792, Robespierre delivered his first address on this subject.

or against an individual; on the contrary, you must adopt a measure of public welfare, achieve an act of national wisdom. In a republic, a dethroned king is a source of danger; he will either endanger the safety of the state and attempt to destroy liberty, or he will take steps to consolidate both.

. . . Our object should be to engrave deep in the hearts of men a contempt for royalty, and to terrify all the King's supporters.

. . . Louis was King and the Republic was founded. The question before you is disposed of by these few words alone. Louis was dethroned by his crimes. Louis denounced the French people as counter-revolutionaries; to conquer them he summoned the armies of the tyrants, his brothers. The victory and the masses have decided that it was he who was the rebel. Louis cannot be judged. He is already condemned, or we have no republic. To propose now that we begin to try Louis XVI would be equivalent to retracing our steps to royal or constitutional despotism. This is a counter-revolutionary idea, for it means nothing more nor less than to indict the Revolution itself. In fact, if it is still possible to make Louis the object of a trial, it is also possible he may be acquitted. He may be not guilty, nay, even more: it may be assumed, before the sentence is pronounced, that he has committed no crime. But if Louis may be declared guiltless, if Louis may go free of punishment, what will then become of the Revolution?

. . . Louis must die in order that the nation may live. In more peaceful times, once we have secured respect and have consolidated ourselves within and without, it might be possible for us to consider generous proposals. But to-day, when we are refused our freedom; to-day, when, after so many bloody struggles, the severity of the law as yet assails only the unhappy; to-day, when it is still possible for the crimes of tyranny to be made a subject of discussion; on such a day there can be no thought of mercy; at such a moment the people cry for vengeance. I request you to come to a decision at once concerning the fate of Louis. . . . Louis XVI must at once be proclaimed by the National Assembly a traitor to the nation, a criminal against mankind, and the judgment must be carried out on the same square on which the great martyrs of freedom died on August 10.

## Report on the Principles of a Revolutionary Government

CITIZENS, members of the Convention! Success induces the weak to sleep, but fills the strong with even more powers of resistance.

Let us leave to Europe and to history the task of lauding the marvels of Toulon, and let us arm for new victories of liberty!

The defenders of the Republic will be guided by Caesar's maxim, and believe that nothing has been accomplished so long as anything remains to be accomplished.

To judge by the power and the will of our republican soldiers, it will be easy to defeat the English and the traitors. But we have another task of no less importance, but unfortunately of greater difficulty. This task is the task of frustrating, by an uninterrupted excess of energy, the eternal intrigues of all enemies of freedom within the country, and of paving the way for the victory of the principles on which the general weal depends.

... The theory of the revolutionary government is as new as the Revolution itself, from which this government was born. This theory may not be found in the books of the political writers who were unable to predict the Revolution, nor in the law books of the tyrants. The revolutionary government is the cause of the fear of the aristocracy, or the pretext for its calumnies. For the tyrants this government is a scandal, for most people it is a miracle. It must be explained to all, so that at least all good citizens may be rallied around the principles of the general weal. . . .

The goal of a constitutional government is the protection of the Republic; that of a revolutionary government is the establishment of the Republic.

The Revolution is the war waged by liberty against its foes—but the Constitution is the regime of victorious and peaceful freedom.

The Revolutionary Government will need to put forth extraordinary activity, because it is at war. It is subject to no constant laws, since the circumstances under which it prevails are those of a storm, and change with every moment. This government is obliged unceasingly to disclose new sources of energy to oppose the rapidly changing face of danger.

Under constitutional rule, it is sufficient to protect individuals against the encroachments of the state power. Under a revolutionary regime, the state power itself must protect itself against all that attack it.

From *Voices of Revolt*, I, 61-70. On 19 Vendemiaire (October 10, 1793), Saint-Just demanded, in the name of the Committee of Public Safety, that the Convention proclaim the Government of the Republic as the revolutionary government up to the conclusion of peace. Robespierre delivered this speech in motivation of this innovation, with which Robespierre was commissioned by the Committee of Public Safety. The speech was then posted publicly in all parishes by the Convention and by the Club of the Jacobins, and was brought to the attention of the Army of the Republic at home and at the front.

The revolutionary government owes a national protection to good citizens; to its foes it owes only death. . . .

Is the revolutionary government, by reason of the greater rapidity of its course and the greater freedom of its movements than are characteristic of an ordinary government, therefore less just and less legitimate? No, it is based on the most sacred of all laws, on the general weal and on the ironclad law of necessity!

This government has nothing in common with anarchy or with disorder; on the contrary, its goal requires the destruction of anarchy and disorder in order to realize a dominion of law. It has nothing in common with autocracy, for it is not inspired by personal passions.

The measure of its strength is the stubbornness and perfidy of its enemies; the more cruelly it proceeds against its enemies, the closer is its intimacy with the republicans; the greater the severities required from it by circumstances, the more must it recoil from unnecessary violations of private interests, unless the latter are demanded by the public necessity. . . .

If we were permitted a choice between an excess of patriotism and a base deficiency in public spirit, or even a morass of moderation, our choice should soon be made. A healthy body, tormented by an excess of strength, has better prospects than a corpse.

Let us beware of slaying patriotism in the delusion that we are healing and moderating it.

By its very nature, patriotism is energetic and enthusiastic. Who can love his country coldly and moderately? Patriotism is the quality of common men who are not always capable of measuring the consequences of all their acts, and where is the patriot to be found who is so enlightened as never to err? If we admit the existence of moderates and cowards who act in good faith, why should there not also exist patriots in good faith, who sometimes err by excess of zeal? If, therefore, we are to regard all those as criminals who have exceeded the limits of caution in the revolutionary movement, we should be obliged to condemn equally the bad citizens, the enemies of the republic, as well as its enthusiastic friends, and should thus destroy the stoutest props of the Republic. There could be no other outcome than that the emissaries of tyranny would be our public prosecutors.

. . . The establishment of the French Revolution was no child's play; it cannot be the work of caprice and carelessness, nor can it be the accidental product of the coalition of all the individual demands and of the revolutionary elements. Wisdom and power created the universe. In assigning to men from your own midst the terrible task of watching over the destinies of our country, you have placed at their disposal your abilities and your confidence. If the revolutionary government is not supported by the intelligence and the patriotism and by the benevolence of all the representatives of the people, where else should it draw the strength enabling it to face the efforts of a united Europe on an equal plane? The authority of the Constituent Assembly must be respected by all Europe. The tyrants are exhausting the resources of their politics, and sacrificing their treasures, in order to degrade this authority and destroy it. The National Assembly, however, prefers its government to the cabinets of London and all the other courts of Europe. Either we shall rule, or the tyrants will rule us. What are the resources of our enemies in this war of treachery and corruption waged by them against the Republic? All the vices fight for them; the Republic has all the virtues on its side. The virtues are simple, poor, often ignorant, sometimes brutal. They are the heritage of the unhappy, the possession of the people. Vice is surrounded by all the treasures, armed with all the charms of voluptuousness, with all the enticements of perfidy; it is escorted by all the dangerous talents that have placed their services at the disposal of crime.

Great skill is shown by the tyrants in turning against us—not to mention our passions and our weaknesses—even our patriotism! No doubt the germs of disunion which they sow among us would be capable of rapid dissemination if we should not hasten to stifle them.

By virtue of five years of treason, by virtue of feeble precautions, and by virtue of our gullibility, Austria, England, Russia and Italy have had time to set up, as it were, a secret government in France, a government that competes with the French government.

. . . Foreign courts have for some time been spewing out on French soil their well-paid criminals. Their agents still infect our armies, as even our victory at Toulon will show. All the bravery of our soldiers, all the devotion of our generals, and all the heroism of the members of this Assembly had to be put forth to defeat treason. These gentlemen still speak in our administrative bodies, in the various sections; they secure admission to the clubs; they sometimes may be found sitting among us; they lead the counter-revolution; they lurk about us, they eavesdrop on our secrets; they flatter our passions and seek even to influence our opinions and to turn our own decisions against us. . . . Blood has flowed all over the country on their account, but we need this blood in the struggle against the tyrants of Europe. . . . We are surrounded by their hired assassins and their spies. We know this, we witness it ourselves, and yet they live! The perfidious emissaries who address us, who flatter us—these are the brothers, the accomplices, the bodyguard of those who destroy our crops, who threaten our cities, massacre our brothers, cut down our prisoners. They are all looking for a leader, even among us. Their chief interest is to incite us to enmity among ourselves. If they succeed in this, this will mean a new lease of life for the aristocracy, the hour of the rebirth of the Federalist plans. . . . We shall continue to make war, war against England, against the Austrians, against all their allies. Our only possible answer to their pamphlets and lies is to destroy them. And we shall know how to hate the enemies of our country.

It is not in the hearts of the poor and the patriots that the fear of terror must dwell, but there in the midst of the camp of the foreign brigands, who would bargain for our skin, who would drink the blood of the French people.

... The conspirators are very numerous. It is far less necessary to punish a hundred unknown, obscure wretches, than to seize and put to death a single leader of the conspirators.

... It is not enough to terrify the enemies of our country; we must also aid its defenders.

We ask that favorable conditions be created for the soldiers who are fighting and dying for liberty.

The French army is not only a terror to the tyrants, it is the glory of humanity and of the nation. In their march to victory, our victorious warriors shout, "Long live the Republic!" They die under the swords of the foe, with the shout, "Long live the Republic!" on their lips; their last words are paeans to liberty, their last gasps are exclamations of homage to their country. If the leaders of the army were as valiant as our soldiers, Europe would have been defeated long ago.

Any measure adopted in favor of the army is an act of national gratitude. . . .

## Report on the Principles of Public Morality

... Having for some time been led often enough by accidents, the representatives of the French people are now beginning to aspire to a political consistency permeated with a strong revolutionary character. Thus far we have been led rather by the storms of circumstances, by our love of the good, by our feeling for the needs of the fatherland, than by any precise theory.

What is the purpose, what is the goal for which we strive? We wish a peaceful enjoyment of freedom and equality, the rule of that eternal justice whose laws are graven not in marble or in stone, but in the hearts of all men. We wish a social order that shall hold in check all base and cruel passions, which shall awaken to life all benevolent and noble impulses, that shall make the noblest ambition that of being useful to our country, that shall draw its honorable distinctions only from equality, in which the generality shall safeguard the wel-

From *Voices of Revolt*, I, 72-75, 77-81. Robespierre, on the instructions of the Committee of Public Safety, delivered this speech on February 5, 1794, in the Convention. It was an attack both on the Right and on the Left.

fare of the individual, and in which all hearts may be moved by any evidence of republican spirit. . . . We want morality in the place of egotism, principles in the place of mere habit, the rule of reason in the place of the slavery of tradition, contempt for vice in the place of contempt for misfortune, the love of glory in the place of avarice. Honest men instead of "good society," truth instead of empty show, manly greatness instead of the depravity of the great, a sublime, powerful, victorious and happy people!

The splendor of the goal pursued by our Revolution is simultaneously the source of our strength and our weakness. It is the source of our weakness, because it unites all the perfidious and vicious individuals, all the advocates of tyranny who think of plunder, who think to find in the Revolution a trade and in the Republic a booty. Thus we may explain the disaffection of many persons who began the struggle together with us, but who have left us when our path was but half accomplished, because they did not pursue the objects we were pursuing. . . .

You are surrounded beyond the boundaries; at home, all the friends of the tyrants conspire, and will continue to conspire, so long as treason still has a hope. We must stifle the domestic and foreign enemies of the Republic, or we must be destroyed with the Republic. And therefore, under the present circumstances, the principle of our Republic is this: to influence the people by the use of reason, to influence our enemies by the use of terror.

In times of peace, virtue is the source from which the government of the people takes it power. During the Revolution, the sources of this power are virtue and terror: virtue, without which terror will be a disaster; and terror, without which virtue is powerless. But terror is nothing more nor less than swift, severe and indomitable justice. . . .

It has been said that terror is the means by which a despotic government rules. Has your rule anything in common with such a government? Yes, indeed, but only in the sense that the sword in the hands of the protagonists of liberty resembles the sword in the hands of the champion of tyranny. When despots rule because their subjects are terrified, the despots are justified—as despots. You put down all the enemies of freedom by means of terror, and you are justified—as founders of the Republic. The government of the Revolution is the despotism of liberty against tyranny. Must might be used only in order to protect crime? . . .

If tyranny prevails for but a single day, all the patriots will have been wiped out by the next morning. And yet some persons dare declare that despotism is justice and that the justice of the people is despotism and rebellion. . . .

Either we or our enemies must succumb. "Show consideration for the Royalists!" shout some persons; "have compassion with the criminal!" "No, I tell you; have compassion with innocence, compassion with the weak, and compassion with humanity! . . ."

The whole task of protecting the Republic is for the advantage of the loyal citizen. In the Republic, only republicans may be citizens. The Royalists and conspirators are foreigners to us, enemies. Is not the terrible war in which we now are involved a single indissoluble struggle? Are the enemies within not the allies of those who attack us from without? The murderers who rend the flesh of their country at home; the intriguers who seek to purchase the conscience of the representatives of the people; the traitors who sell themselves; the pamphleteers who besmirch us and are preparing for a political counter-revolution by means of a moral counter-revolution;—are all these individuals any less dangerous than the tyrants whom they serve? All those who would intervene between these criminals and the sword of justice are like unto those who would throw themselves between the bayonets of our soldiers and the troops of the enemy, and the enthusiasm of their false feelings amounts in my eyes only to sighs directed toward England and Austria!

. . . The internal enemies of the nation have divided into two camps, the camp of the Moderates and the camp of the Counter-Revolutionaries. They are marching on "opposite" paths and under different colors, but they are aiming at the same goal. One of these factions would mislead us into weakness, the other into excess. The one would make of liberty a bacchante, the other a prostitute. The ones have been called "Moderates." The designation of "Ultra-Revolutionaries" perhaps is more brilliant than true. This designation, perhaps appropriate when used of men who, acting in good faith, and ignorant of the facts, have sometimes neglected to practice due caution in the revolutionary policy, is by no means applicable to those perfidious individuals who would compromise us, who would make the principles of the Revolution a plaything to trifle with. The poor revolutionary moves to and fro, straddles, sometimes on either side of the fence. To-day he is a moderate and to-morrow he becomes a fanatic, each time with as little reason. Whenever he discovers anything it is sure to be a plot unveiled long ago; he will tear the mask from the face of traitors who were unmasked long ago, but he will defend the living traitors. He is ever at an effort to adapt himself to the opinions of the moment and never undertakes to oppose them; he is always ready to adopt violent decisions, but he must always be assured in advance that these decisions cannot possibly be carried out; he calumniates those measures that might be fruitful of results, and even if he should approve of them, he will modify them with proposed amendments which would nullify any possible success in advance. Above all, he is very sparing in his use of the truth and resorts to it only as a means to enable him to lie the more shamelessly. High-sounding resolutions find him all fire and flame, but only so long as these resolutions have no real significance. Above all, he is indifferent on any subject that is of importance at the moment; he dotes on the forms of patriotism, the cult of patriotism, and he would rather wear out a hundred red caps than carry out a single revolutionary action.

What is the difference between these people and the Moderate? Both are servants of the same master, servants who maintain that they are hostile to each other, but only in order the better to conceal their misdeeds. Do not judge them by their different language; judge them by the identity of their results. Is he who attacks the Convention publicly in inflammatory speeches any different from him who seeks to deceive and compromise us? Are not these two persons acting in an understanding with each other? . . .

Even the aristocracy is now attempting to make itself popular. It conceals its counter-revolutionary pride, it hides its dagger under its rags and filth. Royalism is trying to overcome the victories of the Republic. The nobility, having learned from past experience, is ready to clasp liberty in a sweet embrace, in order to stifle it in the act. Tyranny strews flowers on the graves of the defenders of liberty. Their hearts have remained the same; only their masks have changed! How many traitors are attempting to ruin us by conducting our affairs?

But they should be put to the test. Instead of oaths and declamations, let us require them to deliver services and sacrifices!

Action is required—they talk. Deliberation is necessary—they declare we must act at once.

. . . It is in this way that these gentlemen serve the Revolution! They have found an excellent means of supporting the efforts of the Republican government: to disorganize us, degrade us, indeed, make war upon those who support us. If you are seeking means for provisioning the army, or if you are engaged in forcing from the hands of avarice and fear the foodstuffs necessary for our warriors—they will shed patriotic tears over the general woe and predict a sure famine. Their alleged desire to avoid the evil is always sufficient reason for them to increase the evil.

. . . It is impossible for you to conceive of all the devious ways pursued by all these sowers of discord, these spreaders of false rumors, who disseminate every possible kind of false report, which is not unprofitable in a country in which, as in ours, superstition is still so widespread . . . .

The domestic situation of our country demands your entire attention. Remember that it is our duty simultaneously to make war against the tyrants of all Europe, to keep fed and equipped an army of 1,200,000 men, and that the government is obliged ceaselessly to keep down with due energy and caution all our internal foes, as well as to repair all our defects. . . .

# louis kossuth

Louis Kossuth was born in Monok, Hungary, on September 19, 1802 and was raised by Lutheran parents. He studied law but failed to obtain a post in the civil service and subsequently found employment as a legal agent, which had been his father's profession, for local landed magnates. It was in this capacity that he attended the Hungarian diets (parliaments) of 1825-27 and 1832-36. As a representative of the landed magnates, he was permitted to sit in the lower house but did not possess the right to speak. During the excited atmosphere of the latter session, the "long diet," Kossuth developed his social and political philosophy. His was one of extreme nationalism combined with advanced radicalism. He embraced many of the liberal reform ideas contemporary to his time, such as taxation of the nobles and the complete emancipation of the peasants, and he held to the belief that no political or social advance would be possible while Hungary remained subordinate to Austria. Intemperate toward those who did not agree with him, Kossuth was blind to the danger involved by too strong a challenge to Vienna, and he frequently treated objections from the Croats or non-Magyars of Hungary as either negligible or treasonable.

Kossuth was arrested in 1837 for his political activities, but popular pressure forced the Metternich regime to release him in 1840. A fiery orator and an accomplished polemicist, Louis Kossuth soon became a popular hero and the editor of a bi-weekly journal, *Pesti Hirlap*. His many articles on political and social subjects were brilliantly written, but they also alarmed the conservative authorities, and Kossuth was forced to resign as editor of the newspaper. Even though he was denied permission to start a journal of his own, Metternich offered him work with the government, an offer Kossuth promptly refused. His next enterprise was to found a society for promoting Hungarian industry, and while this effort realized rather modest economic results, it afforded him a further platform for agitation.

In 1847 the county of Pest sent Kossuth to the diet at Pozsony (Bratislava) where he at once assumed the leadership of the Reform Party. News of the outbreak of revolution in France, in February 1848, provided him with his long-awaited opportunity. On March 3 he delivered a memorable speech demanding the removal of the "dead hand" of Vienna as the only way to safeguard the liberties of Hungary. And when word of the Vienna revolution of March 13 reached Pozsony, he persuaded the Hungarian legislature to accept a program which included the appointment of a responsible ministry for Hungary, together with all of the social reforms favored by the liberals. Moreover, Kossuth accepted the invitation to serve as a member of the Hungarian deputation which carried these demands to Vienna, and much to his satisfaction he saw them all accepted by a panic-stricken Austrian Court.

Count Lajos Batthyany, the new Hungarian prime minister, appointed Kossuth minister of finance, and Kossuth promptly precipitated a crisis by forbidding the exportation of Hungarian revenues owed to the Austrian Crown. Louis Kossuth soon made himself the life and soul of the whole radical and extreme nationalist movement in Hungary. It was he who persuaded the Hungarian diet to refuse, except on political conditions unacceptable to Austria, the dispatch of 20,000 Hungarian troops to Italy. Instead, he called for a national force of 200,000 men to meet the danger of the invasion which he all but invited.

When Austrian armies under the command of Joseph Jellachich invaded Hungary in September of 1848, the government resigned, and Kossuth became *de facto* dictator of Hungary by virtue of his presidency of the committee of national defense. In the absence of a regular government, the diet entrusted the conduct of affairs to this committee, and Kossuth was its dominant officer and personality. Perhaps no one but he could have given the Hungarian people the heart to face the overwhelming odds which faced them (his moving appeal to his countrymen, "Hear! patriots hear!" appears as the first selection which follows); but he also increased those odds by his intransigence and complicated Hungary's own difficulties by his jealousy and suspicion of his best general, Arthur Gorgey, and by his meddling in military affairs. Both his greatness and his lack of realism were manifest in the hours of crisis. It was Kossuth who prevailed upon the

Hungarian diet to refuse recognition of Austrian Emperor Ferdinand's abdication on December 2, 1848, after which he induced the diet to proclaim the dethronement of the Hapsburg dynasty in a declaration issued on April 14, 1849. The diet then proceeded to declare Hungary an independent republic and Kossuth became its president. Military victories in early battles with Austrian troops were cheering to Kossuth, but even he recognized the futility of his cause when the Russian armies entered into an alliance with the Austrians. Kossuth resigned his position in favor of General Gorgey and escaped to Turkey, where authorities kept him interned for two years. The Hungarian surrender at Vilagos marked the end of the republic.

Kossuth was an exile. Before he left Hungary and entered Turkey, he knelt for the last time on his native soil and gave a parting eulogy. His remarks on this occasion appear in the second of the selections from his speeches which follow.

After leaving Turkey, Kossuth travelled to the United States in 1851 where he was received with much popular enthusiasm. The public address which he delivered at the Plymouth Church in Brooklyn, New York (part of which appears as the third selection in the following excerpts from his speeches), was typical of the stirring rhetoric which he invoked during the many appearances of his American tour. Kossuth next travelled to England, where he continued his speaking engagements, always recalling the tragedy of the noble Hungarian cause. (His address at Birmingham, the last of the following selections, is representative of the memorializing speeches which became his hallmark.)

Kossuth never despaired of turning the international situation to Hungary's advantage, but there was little opportunity to do so. His plans for the creation of a Danubian confederation proved equally barren even though he had renounced much of his early chauvinism. In 1865 he moved to Italy where he continued to follow the national movement in Hungary, bitterly denouncing the Compromise of 1867 which established the Austro-Hungarian Monarchy. Kossuth always regarded the unequal status of Hungary, accorded by that Compromise, to be a betrayal of the nationalist cause. He spent his last years in relative seclusion at Turin, Italy, where he died on March 20, 1894. The government permitted his body to be brought back to Hungary and buried at Pest. Louis Kossuth had come home.

## Hear! Patriots Hear!

. . . Hear! patriots hear!

The eternal God doth not manifest himself in passing wonders, but in everlasting laws.

It is an eternal law of God's that whosoever abandoneth himself will be of God forsaken.

It is an eternal law that whosoever assisteth himself him will the Lord assist.

It is a Divine law that swearing falsely is by its results selfchastised.

It is a law of God's that he who resorteth to perjury and injustice, prepareth his own shame and the triumph of the righteous cause.

In the name of that fatherland, betrayed so basely, I charge you to believe my prophecy, and it will be fulfilled.

In what consists Jellachich's power?

In a material force, seemingly mighty, of seventy thousand followers, but of which thirty thousand are furnished by the regulations of the military frontier.

But what is in the rear of this host? By what is it supported? There is nothing to support it!

Where is the population which cheers it with unfeigned enthusiasm? There is none.

Such a host may ravage our territories, but never can subdue us.

Batu-Chan deluged our country with his hundreds of thousands. He devastated, but he could not conquer.

Jellachich's host at worst will prove a locust-swarm, incessantly lessening in its progress till destroyed.

So far as he advances, so far will be diminished the number of his followers, never destined to behold the Drave again.

Let us—Hungarians—be resolved, and stones will suffice to destroy our enemy. This done, it will be time to speak of what further shall befall.

But every Hungarian would be unworthy the sun's light if his first morning thought, and his last thought at eve, did not recall the perjury and treason with which his very banishment from the realms of the living has been plotted.

Thus the Hungarian people has two duties to fulfill.

The first, to rise in masses, and crush the foe invading her paternal soil.

The second, to remember!

If the Hungarian should neglect these duties, he will prove himself dastardly and base. His name will be synonymous with shame and wickedness.

From P. C. Headley, *The Life of Louis Kossuth*, Derby and Miller, Auburn, New York, 1852, pp. 113-115.

So base and dastardly as to have himself disgraced the holy memory of his forefathers—so base, that even his Maker shall repent having created him to dwell upon this earth—so accursed that air shall refuse him its vivifying strength—that the corn-field, rich in blessings, shall grow into a desert beneath his hand—that the refreshing well-head shall dry up at his approach!—Then shall he wander homeless about the world, imploring in vain from compassion the dry bread of charity. The race of strangers for all alms will smite him on the face. Thus will do that stranger-race, which seeks in his own land to degrade him into the outcast, whom every ruffian with impunity may slay like the stray dog—which seeks to sink him into the likeness of the Indian Pariah, whom men pitilessly hound their dogs upon in sport to worry.

For the consolations of religion he shall sigh in vain.

The craven spirit by which Creation has been polluted will find no forgiveness in this world, no pardon in the next.

The maid to whom his eyes are raised shall spurn him from her door like a thing unclean; his wife shall spit contemptuously in his face; his own child shall lisp its first word out in curses on its father.

Terrible! terrible! but such the malediction, if the Hungarian race proves so cowardly as not to disperse the Croatian and Serbian invaders, 'as the wild wind disperses the unbinded sheaves by the way-side.'

But no, this will never be; and, therefore, I say the freedom of Hungary will be achieved by this invasion of Jellachich. Our duty is to triumph first, then to remember.

To arms! Every man to arms; and let the women dig a deep grave between Veszprem and Fehervar, in which to bury either the name, fame, and nationality of Hungary, or our enemy.

And either on this grave will rise a banner, on which shall be inscribed, in record of our shame, 'Thus God chastiseth cowardice;' or we will plant thereon the tree of freedom everlastingly green, and from out whose foliage shall be heard the voice of the Most High, saying, as from the fiery bush to Moses, 'The spot on which thou standest is holy ground.'

All hail! to Hungary, to her freedom, happiness, and fame.

He who has influence in a country, he who has credit in a village, let him raise his banner. Let there be heard upon our boundless plains no music but the solemn strains of the Rakoczy march. Let him collect ten, fifty, a hundred, a thousand followers—as many as he can gather, and marshal them to Veszprem.

Veszprem, where, on its march to meet the enemy, the whole Hungarian people shall assemble, as mankind will be assembled on the Judgment Day.

## Farewell to the Father-Land

God be with thee, my beloved father-land! God be with thee, father-land of the Magyars! God be with thee, land of tortures! I shall not be able to behold the summits of thy mountains; no more shall I be able to call my father-land— the soil, where, on the mother's heart, I imbibed the milk of freedom and justice!

Pardon me, my father-land, me who am condemned to wander about far from thee, because I strove in thy welfare; pardon me, who no more can call any thing *free*, but the small place where I am now kneeling down with a few of thy sons. My looks fall upon thee, O, poor father-land! I see thee bent down with sufferings! I now turn them to futurity; thy future is nothing but a great grief! Thy plains are moistened with crimson gore, which will soon be blackened by unmerciful devastation and destruction, as if to mourn over the many conquests which thy sons have achieved over the accursed enemies of thy hallowed soil. How many grateful hearts lifted up their prayers to the throne of the Almighty! How many tears have flowed, which would even have moved hell to compassion! How many streams of blood have run, as proofs, how the Hungarian loves his father-land, and how he can *die* for it! and yet hast thou, beloved father-land, become a slave!

Thy beloved sons are chained and dragged away like slaves, destined to fetter again every thing that is holy; to become serviceable to all that is unholy! O Lord, if thou lovest thy people, whose heroic ancestors thou didst enable to conquer, under Arpad, amid so manifold dangers, I beseech Thee, and I implore Thee, O humble it not!

Behold, my dear father-land, thus speaks to thee thy son, in the whirlwind of troubles and despair, on thy utmost boundary!

Pardon me, if the great number of thy sons have shed their blood for my sake, or rather for thine, because I was their representative; because I protected thee, when on thy brow was written in letters of blood the word "DANGER!" because I, when it was called unto thee, "Be a slave!" took up the word for thee; because I girded on my sword when the enemy had the audacity to say, "Thou art no more a nation!" in the land of the Magyars!

With gigantic paces time rolled on—with black yellow letters FATE wrote on the pages of thy history "death!" and to stamp the seal upon it, it called the northern Colossus to assist. But the reddening morning dawn of the south will melt this seal!

From Henry W. De Puy, *Kossuth and His Generals,* Phinney & Co., Buffalo, 1852, pp. 284-288.

Behold, my dear father-land, for thee, who hast shed so much of thy blood, there is not even compassion, because on thy hills, which are towered up by the bones of thy sons, tyranny earns her bread.

O see, my dear father-land! the ungrateful, whom thou didst nourish from the fat of thy plenitude, has turned against thee, against thee has turned the traitor, to destroy thee from the head to the sole of thy foot! But thou, noble nation, hast endured all this; thou hast not cursed thy fate, because in thy bosom, over all suffering, HOPE is enshrined.

Magyars! turn your looks not from me; for even at this moment my tears flow only for you, and the soil, on which I am kneeling, yet bears your name!

...I love thee, Europe's truest nation! as I love the freedom for which thou fought so bravely! The God of liberty will never blot you out from His memory. Be blessed for evermore! My principles were those of Washington, though my deeds were not those of William Tell! I wish for a free nation, free as God only can create man—and thou art dead, because thy winter has arrived; but this will not last so long as thy fellow-sufferer, languishing under the sky of Siberia. No, fifteen nations have dug thy grave, the thousands of the sixteenth will arrive, to save thee!

...You may still be proud, for the lion of Europe had to be aroused to conquer the rebels! The whole civilized world has admired you as heroes, and the cause of the heroic nations will be supported by the freest of the free nations on earth!

## Address at Plymouth Church, Brooklyn

... But I am told there are men of peace who say, after all it is very true—very fine, if you please, but they will have peace at any price. Now, I say, there are many things in the world which depend upon true definitions—and it is not true that they are men of peace who speak so—they are men who would conserve, at any price, the present condition of things. Is that present condition peace? Is the scaffold peace?—the scaffold, on which, in Lombardy, the blood of 3,742 patriots was spilled during three short years. Is that peace? Are the prisons of Austria filled with patriots, peace? Or is the blind murmur of discontent from all the nations, peace? I believe the Lord has not created the world to be in such a peaceful condition. I believe he has not created it to be the prison to humanity,

From P. C. Headley, *The Life of Louis Kossuth*, p. 273.

or to be the dominion of the Austrian jailer. No; the present condition of the world is not peace. It is a condition of oppression on the European continent, and because there is this condition of oppression there cannot be peace; for so long as men and nations are oppressed, and so long as men and nations are discontented, there cannot be peace—there can be tranquillity; but it will be the dangerous tranquillity of the volcano, boiling up constantly, and at the slightest opportunity breaking out again, and again, and sweeping away all the artificial props of tranquillity. Freedom is the condition of peace, and, therefore, I will not say that those who profess to be men of peace, and will not help the oppressed to obtain their liberty, are really so. Let them tell truly that they are not men of peace, but only desire to conserve the oppression of nations. With me and with my principles is peace, because I was always a faithful servant of the principles of liberty, and only on the principles of liberty, can nations be contented, and only with the contentment of nations, can there be peace on the earth. With me and with my principles there is peace—lasting peace—consistent peace; with the tyrants of the world there is oppression, struggles, and war.

## Address at Birmingham, England

. . . Perhaps there might be some glory in inspiring such a nation, and to such a degree. But I cannot accept the praise. No; it is not I who inspired the Hungarian people—it was the Hungarian people who inspired me. Whatever I thought, and still think—whatever I felt, and still feel—is but a feeble pulsation of the heart which in the breast of my people beats. The glory of battles is ascribed to the leaders in history; theirs are the laurels of immortality. And yet on meeting the danger, they knew that, alive or dead, their name will upon the lips of the people forever live. How different, how much purer, is the light spread on the image of thousands of the people's sons, who, knowing that where they fall they will lay unknown, their names unhonored and unsung, but who, nevertheless, animated by the love of freedom and fatherland, went on calmly, singing national anthems, against the batteries, whose cross-fire vomited death and destruction on them, and took them without firing a shot—they who fell, falling with the shout, 'Hurrah for Hungary!' And so they died by thousands, THE UNNAMED DEMIGODS! Such is the people of Hungary.

With us, those who beheld the nameless victims of the love of country, lying

From P. C. Headley, *The Life of Louis Kossuth*, pp. 307-308.

on the death-field beneath Buda's walls, met but the impression of a smile on the frozen lips of the dead, and the dying answered those who would console but by the words, 'Never mind, Buda is ours. Hurrah for the fatherland!' So they spoke and died. He who witnessed such scenes, not as exception, but as a constant rule, of thousands of the people:s nameless sons; he who saw the adolescent weep when told he was yet too young to die for his land; he who saw the sacrifices of spontaneity; he who heard what a fury spread over the people on hearing of the catastrophe; he who marked his behavior towards the victors after all was lost; he who knows what sort of curse is mixed in the prayers of the Magyar, and knows what sort of sentiment is burning alike in the breast of the old and of the child, of the strong man and of the tender wife, and ever will be burning on, till the hour of national resurrection strikes; he who is aware of all this, will surely bow before this people with respect, and will acknowledge, with me, that such a people wants not to be inspired, but that it is an everlasting source of inspiration itself.

# giuseppe mazzini

Italian patriot and the guiding revolutionary spirit of the Risorgimento (resurgence), Giuseppe Mazzini was born and raised in Genoa, a city then under French rule. His father was a successful physician who extended his practice to many charity patients; his mother was a public-spirited woman who instilled Mazzini with his republican instincts. A sickly and studious boy, Mazzini obtained his early education under priests with Jansenist leanings, and he became strongly religious yet anticlerical. He attended Genoa University where he studied law, philosophy, medicine, and literature; the latter was his first love. Mazzini graduated in 1827 and in the same year he won acclaim for his essay "Patriotism of Dante," in which he hailed Dante as the prophet of Italian unity.

As a youth Mazzini joined the Carbonari, an illegal Italian revolutionary movement, but soon lost interest in its aimless ritualism. His association with the organization, however, earned him a three-month jail sentence from the Piedmont-Sardinia government in 1831. It was during this confinement that Mazzini completely rejected the Carbonari and formulated his lifetime objective: a united Italy with Rome as its capital. Upon his release, he went into exile and settled for a time in Marseilles. Believing that the future lay in the hands of youth, Mazzini organized *Giovini Italia* (Young Italy), and founded a journal of the same name which was soon printed on secret presses and sold in North and Central Italy. At the prodding of Piedmont authorities, France expelled Mazzini in 1833, and Switzerland did likewise in 1836. In the meantime, Mazzini continued his revolutionary writings and activities (the following selection "Interests and Principles" dates from this period) and he eventually found refuge in 1837 in London, where he spent the greater part of his life.

Doubtlessly Mazzini's influence inspired the many insurrections which finally made Italian nationalism a dynamic force. His chief function in the Risorgimento, in which cause many of his friends were killed in uprisings which occurred between 1833 and 1857, was to venerate the executed as martyrs and to help make nationalism virtually a religion. The Italian insurrections of 1848 brought Mazzini to Italy in April. When the Austrians recaptured Milan, he organized and directed the defense of Rome against French forces seeking to return the exiled Pope Pius IX to his lost throne. Rome was forced to surrender at the end of June, and Mazzini succeeded in escaping to London with the assistance of the United States consul. But the defense of Rome compared so favorably with the humiliating defeat of the Piedmontese army in the north that Mazzini won much respect among Italian nationalists.

After 1849, however, he was less successful. His support of the disastrous revolutions at Mantua in 1852 and at Milan in 1853, weakened his influence. But in London, far from the Italian scene, Mazzini failed to recognize that ordinary people in Italy were not totally committed to nationalism or republicanism. Obstinately refusing to accept any compromise of these goals, he was deserted by Garibaldi and many of his other friends. His letter to Daniele Manin, dated June 8, 1856, and republished here in part, is an example of both this growing alienation and Mazzini's passionate, fervent, and quasi-religious nationalism.

Mazzini rejected socialism because it was too materialistic, too much concerned with rights instead of duties. He aimed for the support of the Italian working class, but he was far too religious and mystical to understand them and was painfully frustrated by their preference for Bakunin's anarchism or Marx's socialism. His relations with Cavour were strained despite their common goal of Italian unification. Cavour relied for help on a foreign power, France, and Mazzini believed in revolution and war based on direct popular action. In 1861 Italy had officially become a nation, but Mazzini was still in exile. Even after the death sentence passed upon him by the Cavour government was removed in 1866, Mazzini could not bring himself to approve Italian unity under the pragmatic Piedmont political leadership. Messina elected him to parliament, but he was prevented from taking his seat because the rulers of the new state did not wish to provoke further controversies. Indeed, Mazzini remained unreconciled even after the capture of Rome in 1870, which, under different circumstances, would have been the climax of his life's dream.

In 1870, he set out for Sicily, but a former associate informed the police and

Mazzini was arrested and imprisoned for several months in Gaeta. He died at Pisa on March 10, 1872, disguised as a Dr. Brown, a fugitive even in his own country.

## Interests and Principles

. . . Every revolution is the work of a principle which has been accepted as a basis of faith. Whether it invoke nationality, liberty, equality, or religion, it always fulfills itself in the name of a principle, that is to say, of a great truth, which, being recognized and approved by the majority of the inhabitants of a country, constitutes a common belief, and sets before the masses a new aim, while authority misrepresents or rejects it. A revolution, violent or peaceful, includes a negation and an affirmation: the negation of an existing order of things, the affirmation of a new order to be substituted for it. A revolution proclaims that the state is rotten; that its machinery no longer meets the needs of the greatest number of the citizens; that its institutions are powerless to direct the general movement; that popular and social thought has passed beyond the vital principle of those institutions; that the new phase in the development of the national faculties finds neither expression nor representation in the official constitution of the country, and that it must therefore create one for itself. This the revolution does create. Since its task is to increase, and not diminish the nation's patrimony, it violates neither the truths that the majority possess, nor the rights they hold sacred; but it reorganizes everything on a new basis; it gathers and harmonizes round the new principle all the elements and forces of the country; it gives a unity of direction toward the new aim, to all those tendencies which before were scattered in the pursuit of different aims. Then the revolution has done its work.

We recognize no other meaning in revolution. If a revolution did not imply a general reorganization by virtue of a social principle; if it did not remove a discord in the elements of a state, and place harmony in its stead; if it did not secure a moral unity; so far from declaring ourselves revolutionists, we should believe it our duty to oppose the revolutionary movement with all our power.

Without the purpose hinted at above, there may be riots, and at times victorious insurrections, but no revolutions. You will have changes of men and administration; one caste succeeding to another; one dynastic branch ousting the other.

From "Interests and Principles, (January 6, 1836)," translated by Thomas Okey, in *The Literature of Italy, 1265-1907*, VI, edited by Rossiter Johnson and Dora K. Ranous, The National Alumni, New York, 1907, pp. 296-300, 303, 305.

This necessitates retreat; a slow reconstruction of the past, which the insurrection had suddenly destroyed; the gradual re-establishment, under new names, of the old order of things, which the people had risen to destroy. Societies have such need of unity that if they miss it in insurrection they turn back to a restoration. Then there is a new discontent, a new struggle, a new explosion. France has proven it abundantly. In 1830 she performed miracles of daring and valor for a negation. She rose to destroy, without positive beliefs, without any definite organic purpose, and thought she had won her end when she canceled the old principle of legitimacy. She descended into that abyss which insurrection alone can never fill; and because she did not recognize how needful is some principle of reconstruction, she finds herself today, six years after the July Revolution, five years after the days of November, two years after the days of April, well on her way to a thorough restoration.

We cite the case of France because she is expected to give political lessons, hopes, and sympathies; and because France is the modern nation in which theories of pure reaction founded on suspicion, on individual right, on liberty alone, are most militant, therefore the practical consequences of her mistakes are shown most convincingly. But twenty other instances might be cited. For fifty years, every movement which, in its turn, was successful as an insurrection, but failed as a revolution, has proven how everything depends on the presence or absence of a principle of reconstruction.

Wherever, in fact, individual rights are exercised without the influence of some great thought that is common to all; wherever individual interests are not harmonized by some organization that is directed by a positive ruling principle, and by the consciousness of a common aim, there must be a tendency for some to usurp others' rights. In a society like ours, where a division into classes, call them what you will, still exists in full strength, every right is bound to clash with another right, envious and mistrustful of it; every interest naturally conflicts with an opposing interest: the landlord's with the peasant's; the manufacturer's or capitalist's with the workman's. All through Europe—since equality, however accepted in theory, has been rejected in practice, and the sum of social wealth has accumulated in the hands of a small number of men, while the masses gain but a mere pittance by their relentless toil—it is a cruel irony, it gives inequality a new lease of life, if you establish unrestricted liberty, and tell men they are free, and bid them use their rights.

A social sphere must have its center; a center to the individualities that jostle with each other inside it; a center to all the scattered rays that diffuse and waste their light and heat. The theory that bases the social structure on individual interests cannot supply this center. The absence of a center, or the selection among opposing interests of that which has the most vigorous life, means either anarchy or privilege—that is, either barren strife or the germ of aristocracy, under whatever name it disguises itself: this is the parting of the ways, which it is impossible to avoid.

Is this what we want when we invoke a revolution, since a revolution is indispensable to reorganize our nationality?

. . . We are therefore driven to the sphere of principles. We must revive belief in them; we must fulfill a work of faith. The logic of things demands it.

Principles alone are constructive. Ideals are never translated into facts without the general recognition of some strong belief. Great things are never done except by the rejection of individualism and a constant sacrifice of self to the common progress. Self-sacrifice is the sense of duty in action. . . . The individual is sacred; his interests, his rights are inviolable. But to make them the only foundation of the political structure, and tell each individual to win his future with his own unaided strength, is to surrender society and progress to the accidents of chance and the vicissitudes of a never-ending struggle; to neglect the great fact of man's nature, his social instinct; to plant egotism in the soul; and in the long run impose the dominion of the strong over the weak, of those who have over those who have not. The many futile attempts of the past forty years prove this.

. . . If by dint of example you can root in a nation's heart the principle that the French Revolution proclaimed but never carried out, that the State owes every member the means of existence or the chance to work for it, and add a fair definition of existence, you have prepared the triumph of right over privilege; the end of the monopoly of one class over another, and the end of pauperism; for which at present there are only palliatives . . . Christian charity, or cold and brutal maxims like those of the English school of political economists.

When you have raised men's minds to believe in the other principle—that society is an association of laborers—and can, thanks to that belief, deduce both in theory and practice all its consequences; you will have no more castes, no more aristocracies, or civil wars, or crises. You will have a People.

## To Daniele Manin (June 8, 1856)

Daniele Manin was an Italian patriot and statesman. He became head of the Venetian Republic in 1848 but resigned the same year when Venice voted in

From *Mazzini's Letters*, translated by Alice De Rosen Jervis, J.M. Dent and Sons, Ltd., London, 1930, pp. 152, 154-163.

favor of union with the kingdom of Sardinia. In 1849, Manin again became head of a provisional government and after the Sardinian rout at Novara he was given dictatorial powers and organized a heroic resistance of Venice to its Austrian besiegers. Famine and disease forced Venice to surrender in August, 1849, whereupon Manin went into exile at Paris. He subsequently supported the leadership of Sardinia in the movement for Italian unification.

. . . One of your last letters, under the pretext of a moral lesson, has brought such an accusation against the party, that to leave it unrefuted would appear like indifference or agreement. Therefore I am writing to you.

In that letter you assert that the party will never succeed in its patriotic enterprise, unless it formally abjures the *theory of the dagger.*

. . .I have been told by some that, in denouncing the *theory of the dagger,* you pointed indirectly at me, without mentioning my name, at me and the men who are associated with me in the idea of action. I do not believe that you have a mean mind, and I reject the suspicion. But how was it that the affection owed to him, who has been fighting for the Italian cause for more than twenty-five years, did not suggest to you that others might interpret your words in this sense? How was it that you did not remember that the governments and journals of the *moderate* party in Piedmont and Lombardy, and *The Times,* depositary of your thoughts, had vied with each other in spreading this cowardly accusation against me, after the 6th February,1853? How was it that it did not occur to you that in haranguing against the *theory of the dagger* you were supporting—in discourteous forgetfulness—the calumnies of spies, credulous people, and unconscientious enemies, who imputed to me death-sentences, secret tribunals, and tendencies to illegal revenge?

And yet, it is not in my own name—it matters little to me now whether the opinion of others be good or bad, unless it is that of those whom I love—but in the name of a whole party, that I ask you solemnly: when was the *theory of the dagger* sanctioned in Italy? Who spread it? Who supported it by word or deed?

If by *theory of the dagger* you mean the language of him who cries to a subjugated people, without a country, without a banner to spread over its sons in the cradle or the grave: "Rise up: slay or die: you are not men, but tools employed at pleasure by the foreigner; you are not a people, but a disinherited race of slaves, despised all the more when you whine; you are not Italians, but Israelites, Pariahs, the Helots of Europe; you have no name, no national baptism, but are merely a number; you are represented by a cipher, and the Emperor Francis I brutally used one to describe some of our finest men sighing, tortured and crushed, in the secret cells of the Spielberg. Your one and only duty is to become men and citizens; all education begins with this: no progress can start except from what already exists; *rise up* then and *exist;* rise up mightily against all who by brute force impede you from following the way taught you by Providence; rise up, in sublime fury. If your oppressors have disarmed you, create arms with which to fight them; let your weapons of war be the iron of your crosses, the nails from your workshops, the pebbles of your streets, the daggers with which a file can furnish you. Conquer by artifice and surprise the arms with which the foreigner deprives you of honour, substance, liberty, rights, and life. From the dagger of the Vespers to the stone of Balilla, and the knife of Palafox, blessed by everything which can destroy the enemy and emancipate you."—This language is mine, and ought to be yours.

. . . But if by *theory of the dagger* you mean the language of him who would say to our fellow-citizens: "Strike, not to begin an insurrection, but with the sole intent of striking, and because you do not wish or are not able to rise in insurrection; strike in the dark; strike isolated individuals, whose life is not an obstacle to the Country nor their death a deliverance for it; substitute revenge, which dishonours, for the conspiracy, which emancipates; form yourselves into a tribunal before being citizens, and before being able to concede to the victim time for repentance or justification." Who has held such language? Who has spread such an atrocious theory in Italy? It is your duty to say this, or to retract the accusation.

. . . The theory of the dagger subsists in this: in the insane, incessant, and cruel persecution of thought, and of the smallest acts which give rise to suspicion in those who are guilty, or believed to be guilty, of affection for their Country, their substance being forfeited and their lives threatened—in flogging taking the place of law in Italy—in the perpetual insolence of the foreign rulers—in the feverish irritation caused by the orders given out and by the shameful espionage—in the hatreds aroused by paid denunciations—in the overbearing deeds perpetrated (under cover of a Government abhorred like the Papal Government), by tyrannical underlings known to everyone in our small cities—in the unavoidable scorn for every existing institution—in the impossibility of obtaining justice against the extortions of the oppressors—in the contempt of life (an inevitable consequence of the uncertainty of the future)—in a condition of things which depends solely upon the despotism of those in power—in the culpable indifference of the Governments of Europe to our idea of a common Country, this immense aspiration of ours, nourished and repressed for half a century.

The party, collectively, has always rejected the great temptation that our oppressors place before us. If a few individuals, acting only upon their own initiative, now and then succumb, the fact is a result of the causes which I have pointed out, and it will not cease except with their cessation. You ought to have said this. You ought to have reminded Europe how, in every part of Italy, our people has been sublime in pardon and oblivion, whenever it had a ray of freedom. You ought to have reminded her how, only yesterday, an English minister, contradicting himself, declared in the House of Commons, concerning Rome, that our cities were never so well governed or so free from crime and violence as when a banner of the Country floated over their towers. You ought to have re-evoked the picture of our wretched conditions, and to have cried: *"The Austrian Government, which, against the unanimous vote of the popu-lation, persists in keeping what does not belong to it; the French Government, which deprived Rome of every means of amelioration; the Protestant English Government, which declared in its dispatches that it desired the return of the Pope; the Governments of all Europe, which forbid Italy to be a Nation—are responsible before God and man for the daggers that flash through the darkness of our land. They all conspire to prevent our free development, and to maintain a great injustice upon our soil: let them blame themselves if an abnormal and violent protest should sometimes issue from an enslaved and uneducated people, who are abandoned by all."*

It seems to me that this should have been your part. To cry to the men who are agonizing unjustly under the knife of the executioner: *"do not use the knife which falls into your hands,"* is the same as crying to one who is dying in a vitiated atmosphere: *"let the blood circulate freely through your veins, and you will be cured."* It is the same error as that of the worthy men who wait to initiate the republican institution, till those born and bred under monarchical despotism develop republican virtues.

The *theory of the dagger* has never existed in Italy; the *fact* of the dagger will disappear when Italy has her own life, recognized rights, and justice.

To-day, I do not approve, I deplore; but I have not the heart to condemn. When a man, Vandoni, at Milan, cunningly persuades one of his old friends to accept from him a ticket in the National Loan, and then hastens to denounce him to the foreign police, if a man of the people rises the next day and stabs the Judas at noon in the public thoroughfare, I have not the courage to cast a stone at this man who makes himself a representative of social justice, hated by tyranny.

I abhor a single drop of blood being shed, when not imperatively required for the triumph or the consecration of a sacred principle. I believe the death-sentence to be a crime when applied by a society which can defend itself, and it is my earnest desire that the first decree of the triumphant republic may be the abolition of the gallows. I sigh over individual acts of vengeance, even when against iniquitous persons, and even when every means of legal justice is wanting where they are committed. Braving the accusation of weakness, I refused to append my signature to a sentence of death pronounced by a tribunal of war against a guilty soldier. Therefore I do not fear a wrong interpretation being put upon my words by honest people, if I add that there are exceptional moments, both in life and in the history of nations, to which normal human justice cannot adapt itself, and when men can only act as their conscience and God inspire them.

The sword in Judith's hand which destroyed Holophernes was sacred; the dagger of Brutus, the stiletto of the Sicilian who started the Vespers, and the arrow of Tell, were sacred. Where all Justice is dead, and a tyrant denies and destroys by terrorism the conscience of a nation towards God who willed it to be free—and a man, without hatred or base passion, but actuated only by devotion to his Country and the eternal right which he embodies, arises to confront the tyrant, crying: *thou tormentest millions of my brothers; thou deprivest them of that which was given them by God; thou slayest their bodies and corruptest their souls; thou condemnest my countrymen to live in agony day after day; in thee is embodied the whole edifice of servitude, dishonour, and guilt: therefore I destroy this edifice in slaying thee*—I recognize the finger of God in that manifestation of tremendous equality between the ruler of millions and a single individual. Most men feel as I do in their hearts, but I acknowledge it.

Therefore I will not cry anathema, like you, Manin, on these assailants; I will not say to them, with evident injustice: *you are cowards*; I will not say to the party, which never encourages these deeds: *you will fail in your object, if you do not stop them;* but I will say: "Why do you strike, wretched men? What do you hope for? If ever man has a right to take the life of another, I know that death is deserved by the spy and the traitor, and by the vile Italian who in return for money from the foreign oppressor accepts the infamous mission of torturing at the gallows his brothers who were intolerant of the Country's servitude; but what is the use of slaying them, and can you slay them all? And can you, unaided, be judges of what is stirring in the conscience of your victim? Do you know whether he will not repent and be better to-morrow? Anyway, do you wish to be as bad as he is? To conquer, we must be better; to deserve the victory, we must drive anger, ferocity, and vengeance, out of our hearts. We are the apostles of the future Country, and wish to found a Nation. In this sacred idea, and in the duty of making it triumph, lies the source of our rights. Now can you found a Nation and conquer a Country in this way?

"It is your business to slay, not a few satellites of your tyrants, but tyranny itself. As long as tyranny exists, as long as there are corrupt rulers, foreign bayonets, and the gallows, there will also be corrupt and servile people, cowardly traitors, torturers, and executioners. And they will always spring up afresh, because your dagger flashes rarely and uncertainly, whilst the bayonet of the oppressors shines steadily before everyone's eyes, inexorable and omnipotent. Concentrate your energy, then, in an idea of collective insurrection, which may free your soil at one blow from the causes that create vile and cowardly men. In concord amongst yourselves, turn your weapons against the foreign invaders, instead of assuming the solemn office of judges—without allowing examination of defence—and using them against men who are merely tools of the tyranny which rules over you. When once you are free, you need not fear or punish traitors or iniquitous judges. The right of conquering your Country for yourselves is a right given you by God; that which you derogate to yourselves against individuals who are the blind agents of despotism sways between justice and crime."

These men might allow me to use this language to them, because I cry: *Rise up!* and point out the only simple and rational way of doing so, making it possible as far as I can, accepting and invoking the fraternal co-operation of everyone, and summoning all Italians to unite and to work in concord, with a programme which no one can refuse without intolerance or treachery to the common Country: *Let the Nation deliver the Nation: Let the Nation, free and united, decide its destiny.* But you?

Place your hand on your heart, and answer me: if one of those men upon whom you call down anathema were to rise up and say: "Daniele Manin, you, amongst others, preached hatred of the foreign rule, national unity, and abhorrence of the Italians who deny our faith. You, amongst others, put the fever for our Country into our souls. Why do you not join with the others to guide us to the conquest of that ideal? Why do you leave us alone? Why, instead of turning to us, your brothers, do you turn to diplomacy, to foreign courts, and to a monarchy which does not wish and is not able to save us? There are millions of us; we have proved in 1848 and 1849 that we are capable of emancipating our soil; we are stronger now than we were then, and the very facts which you blame show it you; why do you not help us in the work of common redemption, which we shall certainly undertake? Why do not you and the others whom we hailed as our leaders, and whom we are still ready to hail as such, unite with those who are working for us? You do not like our daggers: why do you not give us muskets? You could do so; if you and a dozen others whose names are dear to all were to join in saying openly and boldly: "the hour has arrived"; were to join in asking wealthy people to give part of their substance to help us, who place our lives in the balance, you would succeed in convincing and in inducing to make sacrifices those who are now wavering irresolutely amidst the disorder of the party. Why do you not do this? Why do you draw us on from one illusion to another, until we are overwhelmed by despair? Do you expect the European Powers to come to be slain for our sake? Do you wish the emancipation of Italy to be accomplished by foreign forces? No; join us openly and frankly. Join your intellect to our strong arms. Then only will you have the right to advise us." What answer could you make to such language?

# giuseppe garibaldi

Italian patriot and guerrilla leader of the Risorgimento (resurgence), Garibaldi was a republican who by his conquest of Sicily and Naples greatly contributed to the achievement of Italian unity under the royal house of Savoy. Born on July 4, 1807, at Nice, then a French town but from 1815 to 1860 included in the kingdom of Sardinia-Piedmont, Garibaldi entered the Sardinian navy in 1833. After meeting Giuseppe Mazzini, the pre-eminent Italian nationalist of that day, he joined *Giovini Italia* (Young Italy). In 1834, he became involved in an unsuccessful republican plot in Piedmont and was forced to flee to South America the following year. There he gained his first experience in irregular warfare. He fought primarily at sea on behalf of partisans in Brazil, and on behalf of Uruguay against Argentina. In 1843, however, he helped form an Italian legion, the first "Redshirts," with whom he gained much of his experience of guerrilla warfare. It was in Uruguay that he met Anna Maria Ribeiro da Silva, known as Anita, whom he married in 1842. She accompanied him on his expeditions and became a figure only less legendary than Garibaldi himself.

When revolution swept over Europe in 1848, Garibaldi found a new theatre of action. Although a convinced republican, he offered his services to King Charles Albert of Sardinia in the war against Austria but received no encouragement. After the Sardinian defeat at Custozza, Garibaldi led a small guerrilla band and harassed the Austrians in the area around lakes Maggiore and Varese. From there he travelled to Rome in 1849 and, at the head of some improvised forces, fought for Mazzini's short-lived Roman republic against the French forces intervening for Pope Pius IX. The bravery and tenacity of the defenders at Rome, at a time when other revolutionaries were offering but feeble resistance to the return of the old regimes, proved to the world that Italians could and would fight for national freedom. During Garibaldi's spectacular retreat across central Italy, Anita died. Garibaldi was refused asylum by the king of Sardinia and came to the United States where he resumed his seafaring life.

Permitted to return to Sardinia in 1854, Garibaldi bought part of the island of Paprera, lying between Corsica and Sardinia, with the intention of retiring. By this date he had renounced the dream of an Italian republic and gave his support to the pragmatic policies of Cavour, publicly declaring that the monarchy as represented by Sardinian King Victor Emmanuel II should be the basis of Italian unity. Garibaldi's popularity won many of Mazzini's republican followers for the monarchist cause. Indeed, Garibaldi was made a major general in the Sardinian army and was placed in charge of a brigade of "volunteers" in the war of 1859 against Austria. After the Treaty of Villafranca di Verona he violently attacked Cavour and denounced the cession of Savoy and his native Nice to France.

The greatest exploit of his life was the expedition to Sicily and Naples (May-November, 1860), which he undertook with the connivance of Victor Emmanuel. He set sail from the Genoese coast on May 6, with the object of assisting a revolt in Sicily. His force consisted then of just more than 1,000 volunteers and is therefore known as "the Thousand." Insofar as they had a uniform, it was the red shirt. On May 11 they reached Marsala, and Garibaldi was proclaimed dictator of Sicily in the name of King Victor Emmanuel. The campaign in Sicily was astonishingly successful, and, after the capitulation of the Neapolitan forces garrisoned in Sicily, Garibaldi crossed the strait of Messina on the night of August 18, 1860. On September 7 he entered Naples as the Sardinian army marched south against the Papal States. Garibaldi held the line against powerful Neapolitan forces along the Volturno River until the Sardinians arrived on October 26. When King Victor Emmanuel II made his triumphal entry into Naples on November 7, Garibaldi was with him. But two days later he returned to Caprera, refusing any reward.

Only a part of the Papal States remained outside the new kingdom, and Garibaldi decided to liberate the area without reference to Victor Emmanuel. Garibaldi expected to be able to complete the unification of Italy in the same unconventional fashion in which he had begun, but the King, fearing international intervention, sent an Italian army which defeated Garibaldi at Aspromonte. Wounded and then captured, he was quickly freed. During his convalescence Garibaldi paid a visit to London, in April 1864, where he received an unparalleled welcome. In the war of 1866 he was allowed a subsidiary role in the effort against the Austrians, which he performed well. Then in 1867 he embarked on another expedition to Rome. He was arrested and sent back to Caprera, which the Italian navy proceeded to blockade. He eluded his guard, however, and made a final attempt to seize Rome in 1867. On November 2, his forces were defeated at Mentana by French and papal troops. Recrossing the Italian frontier, he was again arrested and taken back to his island.

In 1870 Garibaldi formed a fresh volunteer corps, this time to assist France against Prussia. For this service he was rewarded by his election to the Bordeaux national assembly. But parliamentary life was ill-suited to his temperament, and he soon resigned. He lived most of the rest of his life in retirement and died at Caprera on June 2, 1882.

Garibaldi was not without serious shortcomings for all of his accomplishments. He was not intellectually oriented: he did not think and argue; he believed and declaimed. In some ways he presaged the twentieth century dictators. He distrusted parliaments because he did not understand politics and so usually made a fool of himself when he participated in the national assembly. Yet he was no bad ruler. It is arguable that he provided better government with his simple minded radicalism when he was dictator of Sicily and Naples than the Kingdom of Italy was to provide with its subtle conservatism. He was, however, a soldier, and there was perhaps no greater master of guerrilla warfare in the nineteenth century.

Garibaldi never lacked admirers. During his lifetime he attracted an almost fanatical devotion that extended well beyond the borders of Italy to a world which worshipped romance and heroism. In America and England, just as in Italy, the working classes identified with him and hailed his career as a promise of a better world to come. His simple eloquence, evidenced in the edited selections which follow, impressed Gandhi and suggested to Jawaharlal Nehru how an idealistic and unselfish patriotism might triumph over seemingly impossible difficulties and bring a new nation to birth. Garibaldi gave the world a Latin heart.

## The Sicilian Campaign, May 1860

SICILY! a filial and well-merited affection makes me consecrate these first words of a glorious period to thee, the land of marvels and of marvellous men. The mother of Archimedes, thy glorious history bears the impress of two achievements paralleled in that of no other nation on earth, however great—two achievements of valour and genius, the first of which proves that there is no tyranny, however firmly constituted, which may not be overthrown in the dust, crushed into nothingness by the dash, the heroism, of a people like thine, intolerant of outrages.

. . . Once more, Sicily, it was thine to awaken sleepers, to drag them from the lethargy in which the stupefying poison of diplomatists and doctrinaires had sunk them—slumberers who, clad in armour not their own, confided to others the safety of their country, thus keeping her dependent and degraded.

Austria is powerful, her armies are numerous; several formidable neighbours are opposed, on account of petty dynastic aims, to the resurrection of Italy. The Bourbon has a hundred thousand soldiers. Yet what matter? The heart of twenty-five millions throbs and trembles with the love of their country! Sicily, coming forward as champion and representative of these millions, impatient of servitude, has thrown down the gauntlet to tyranny, and defies it everywhere, combating it alike within convent walls and on the peaks of her ever-active volcanoes. But her heroes are few, while the ranks of the tyrant are numerous; and the patriots are scattered, driven from the capital, and forced to take to the mountains. But are not the mountains the refuge, the sanctuary, of the liberty of nations? The Americans, the Swiss, the Greeks, held the mountains when overpowered by the ordered cohorts of their oppressors. "Liberty never escapes those who truly desire to win her." Well has this been proved true by those resolute islanders, who, driven from the cities, kept up the sacred fire in the mountains. Weariness, hardships, sacrifices—what do they matter, when men are fighting for the sacred cause of their country, of humanity?

O noble Thousand! in these days of shame and misery, I love to remember you! Turning to you, the mind feels itself rise above this mephitic atmosphere of robbery and intrigue, relieved to remember that, though the majority of your gallant band have scattered their bones over the battle-fields of liberty, there yet remain enough to represent you, ever ready to prove to your insolent detractors that all are not traitors and cowards—all are not shameless self-seekers, in this land of tyrants and slaves! "Where any of our brothers are fighting for liberty,

From *Autobiography of Giuseppe Garibaldi*, II, translated by A. Werner, Walter Smith and Innes, London, 1889, pp. 143-147.

thither all Italians must hasten!"—such was your motto, and you hastened to the spot without asking whether your foes were few or many, whether the number of true men was sufficient, whether you had the means for the arduous enterprise. You hastened, defying the elements, despising difficulties and dangers and the obstacles thrown in your way by enemies and self-styled friends. In vain did the numerous cruisers of the Bourbon armament surround as with a circle of iron the island about to shake off their yoke; in vain they ploughed the Tyrrhene seas in all directions, to overwhelm you in their abysses—in vain! Sail on, sail on, argonauts of Liberty!

. . . Yet sail on, sail on fearlessly, *Piemonte* and *Lombardo*, [The two steamers which carried the Thousand to Marsala], noble vessels manned by the noblest of crews; history will remember your illustrious names in despite of calumny. And when the survivors of the Thousand, the last spared by the scythe of time, sitting by their own fireside, shall tell their grandchildren of the expedition—mythical as it will seem in those days—in which they were found worthy to share, they will recall to the astonished youth the glorious names of the vessels which composed it.

Sail on! sail on! Ye bear the Thousand, who in later days will become a million—in the day when the blindfolded masses shall understand that the priest is an impostor, and tyrannies a monster anachronism. How glorious were thy Thousand, O Italy, fighting against the plumed and gilded agents of despotism, and driving them before them like sheep!—glorious in their motley array, just as they came from their offices and workshops, at the trupet-call of duty—in the student's coat and hat, or the more modest garb of the mason, the carpenter, or the smith.

### Address to the People of Palermo

People of Palermo!—Your aspirations are those of the whole peninsula. Let all Italians be unanimous in one will—the unity of the country. But let us have no words; let us have deeds and protests—not in writing—the protests of a brave people determined to free their brethren still groaning in fetters. The master of France, the traitor of the 2nd of December, under the pretence of screening from harm the person of the Pope, of protecting religion, Catholicism, occupies Rome. It is a false pretence—or lie. . . . He is actuated by covetousness, by a

From *The Times* (London), July 17, 1862, p. 12.

robber's lust, by an infamous thirst for empire; he is the first supporter of brigandage! the chief of Southern assassins!

People of the Vespers! people of 1860! Napoleon must depart from Rome. If it be necessary, we must resort to a new rehearsal of the Vespers. Let every citizen who cares for the emancipation of the country have a weapon in readiness (*un ferro* a sword or dagger). Strong and compact, we shall be able to overcome the greatest power.

. . . The Pope-King, or the King-Pope, is a negation of Italy. Our Government is not strong enough to shake off the yoke of France. The people must strengthen them by its compactness and energy. Let us throw our well-sharpened weapons into the scales of diplomacy, and diplomacy will respect our rights; she will give us Rome and Venice.

The programme with which we crossed the Ticino and landed at Marsala must still be 'Italy and Victor Emmanuel.' The same programme will lead us to Rome and Venice.

I will rouse Italy from the sloth in which she is lying. I will come with you; I will be your companion, in this last struggle. Once more I recommend concord; we must avoid intestine war. All of us have committed errors, but all of us wish for the emancipation of Italy. If we disagree in some things, it matters not so we are all brethren.

## Proclamation to the Volunteers at Bois Fienzi

My young fellow-soldiers,—Again to-day the holy cause of our country reunites us. Again to-day, without asking whither going, what to do, with what hope of reward to our labours, with a smile on your lips and joy in your hearts, you hastened to fight our overbearing dominators, throwing a spark of comfort to our enslaved brethren. I only ask of Providence to strengthen your good trust in me and make me worthy of it. Such is and ever was the desire of my whole life. I can only promise you toils, hardships, and perils; but I rely on your self-denial. I know you, ye brave young men, crippled in glorious combat. It is idle to beg you to display valour in fight. What I ask is discipline, for without that no army can exist. The Romans were disciplined, and they mastered the world. Endeavour to conciliate the good will of the population we are about to visit, as you did in 1860, and no less to win the esteem of our valiant army, in order, thus gaited

From *The Times* (London), August 6, 1862, p. 9.

with that army, to bring about the longed-for unity of the country. This time, again, the brave Sicilians will be the forerunners of the great destinies which are in store for our country.

## Appeal to the Hungarians

Hungarians!—What is Hungary about? Is that noble nation, which already the victorious Turk has seen rise suddenly armed in the defence of the civilization of Europe—that nation before which the proud Emperors of Hapsburg have bent as supplicants, asking aid and mercy—is it gone to sleep for ever?

Brothers of Hungary! Revolution is on your threshold. Sharpen your glance, and you will see the flag of liberty floating on the towers of Belgrade. Listen attentively, and you will hear the rattle of Servian rifles, who, up and armed in defence of their rights, are fighting against the abhorred system.

And you,—what are you about? You, a strong people, who have not had the misfortune, which Italy once suffered, of being divided between seven tyrants—you, a people of warriors, what are you waiting for? Have you broken your swords? Have you forgotten your martyrs, renounced your vows of vengeance, or do you rely on the perfidious promises of your oppressors? Do you put faith in those who advise you to accept the insidious offers of Austria, who seems inclined now to grant you your rights, but who is already preparing to betray you, and to take from you by force or fraud what she reluctantly gives you?

... You also are oppressed under a ferocious despotism; you also have Austria like a rock on your chest, stopping your breath—Austria, whose empire you have saved more than once—Austria, who, as a reward for having lent her many a time the bulwark of your powerful breasts, has violated your laws, annihilated your statutes, attempted to abolish your language, exiled your best citizens, and erected gallows in your cities! Do you despair of your own strength and valour! Do not forget that in 1848 you had only to push on your triumphal road to Vienna to destroy for ever the old sanguinary throne of the Hapsburgs.

The present moment is more propitious. Russia will not now offer a helping hand to Austria to thwart your efforts; she has been paid with too much ingratitude; and Prussia, the ancient rival of the Empire, will not defend her against your attacks.

Woe to Hungary!—woe to every oppressed people—if you obey fallacious and

From *The Times* (London), August 27, 1862, p. 9.

cowardly counsels, if you think any other pact between you and Austria possible
except hatred and war! Oh, brothers! do not miss this propitious opportunity.

. . . And you. . . you want liberty. You. . . oppressed and outraged, you have
the right—more than the right—the duty of reasserting the rank earned by your
glorious deeds, your virtues, and the services which you have rendered to civilization.

. . . Courage! You have sufficient strength if you have sufficient daring.
Hearken not to those who counsel patience and an ignominious servility, but
listen to the voice of your conscience, which says, 'Up! follow the example of
Servia and of Montenegro; imitate those who are ready to apply the torch of
revolution on other points of Europe.'

Italy, who loves you as brothers, who has promised to repay you the price of
blood which your brave sons have shed for her on many battle-fields—
Italy,. . . calls upon you to share her new battles and her new victories over
despotism; she invokes you, in the name of the holy fraternity of peoples, in the
name of the welfare of all.

. . Will you fail to join the rendezvous of nations when they meet to do battle
against despotism? Certainly liberty abandoned by you would run great risks;
but your fame would be lost for ever.

. . . Oh! I know you! I do not doubt you. Hungary, too long deceived by
perfidious friends, will awaken to the cry of liberty, which to-day reaches it
across the Danube, and will to-morrow resound from Italy. And when the
solemn hour of nations strikes I shall, I am sure, meet your invincible phalanxes
on that field where a death-struggle will be fought between liberty and tyranny,
between barbarism and civilization.

Palermo, July 26, 1862

## To the English Nation

Suffering under repeated blows, both moral and physical, a man can more
exquisitely feel both good and ill, hurl a malediction at the authors of evil, and
consecrate to his benefactors unlimited gratitude and affection.

And I owe you gratitude, O English nation! and I feel it as much as my soul is
capable of feeling it. You were my friend in my good fortune, and you will

From *The Times* (London), October 3, 1862, p. 7.

continue your precious friendship to me in my adversity. May God bless you. My gratitude is all the more intense, O kind nation! that it rises high above all individual feeling, and becomes sublime in the universal sentiment towards nations of which you represent the progress. Yes, you deserve the gratitude of the world, because you offer a safe shelter to the unfortunate from whatever side they may come, and you identify yourself with the misfortunes of others you pity and help. The French or Neapolitan exile finds refuge in your bosom against tyranny. He finds sympathy and aid because he is an exile, because he is unfortunate. The Haynaus, the iron executioners of autocrats, will not be supported by the soil of your free country; they will fly from the tyrannicidal anger of your generous sons.

And what should we be in Europe without your dignified behaviour! Autocracy can strike her exiled ones in other countries where only a bastard freedom is enjoyed—where freedom is but a lie. But let one seek for it on the sacred ground of Albion. I, like so many others, seeing the cause of justice oppressed in so many parts of the world, despair of all human progress. But when I turn my thoughts to you, I find tranquillity from your steady and fearless advancement towards that end to which the human race seems to be called by Providence.

Follow your path undisturbed, O unconquered nation! and be not backward in calling sister nations on the road of human progress. Call the French nation to co-operate with you. You are both worthy to walk hand in hand in the front rank of human improvement. But call her! In all your meetings let the words of concord of the two great sisters rebound. Call her! Call her in every way with your own voices, and with that of her great exiles—with that of her Victor Hugo, the hierophant of sacred brotherhood. Tell her that conquests are to-day an aberration, the emanation of insane minds. And why should we conquer foreign lands when we must all be brothers? Call her, and do not care if she is for the moment under the dominion of the Spirit of Evil. She will answer in due time, if not to-day, to-morrow, and, if not to-morrow, she will later answer to the sound of your generous and regenerating words. Call, and at once, Helvetia's strong sons and clasp them for ever to your heart. The warrior sons of the Alps—the Vestals of the sacred fire of freedom in the European Continent, they will be yours! And what allies! Call the great American Republic. She is, after all, your daughter, risen from your bosom; and, however she may go to work, she is struggling to-day for the abolition of slavery so generously proclaimed by you. Aid her to come out from the terrible struggle in which she is involved by the traffickers in human flesh. Help her, and then make her sit by your side, in the great assembly of nations, the final work of human reason. Call unto you such nations as possess free will, and do not delay a day. The initiative that to-day belongs to you might not be yours to-morrow. May God avert this! Who more bravely took the initiative than France in 1789. She who in that solemn moment gave to the world the goddess Reason, levelled tyranny to the dust, and consecrated free brotherhood between nations. After almost a century she is reduced to combat the liberty of nations, to protect tyranny, and to direct her efforts to steady, on the ruins of the temple of Reason, that hideous, immoral monstrosity—the Papacy. Rise, therefore, O Britannia! and lose no time. Rise with uplifted brow and point out to other nations the road to follow. War would no longer be possible where a world's Congress would judge of the differences arisen between nations. No more standing armies, with which freedom is incompatible! Away with shells and iron plating! Let spades and reaping machines come forth; let the millards [billions] spent in destructive implements be employed to encourage industry and to diminish the sum of human misery. Begin, O English people! for the love of God begin the great era of the human compact, and benefit present generations with so great a gift.

Besides Switzerland, Belgium, and others that will rise at your call, you will see other nations, urged on by the good sense of their populations, rush to your embrace and unite in one. Let London be at the present time the seat of the Congress, in due course to be chosen by mutual understanding and general consent. I repeat to you, may God bless you, and may He amply repay you for the benefits you have showered upon me.

Varignano, Sept. 28, [1862]

## Proclamation to the Italian People

Before the hypocritical intrigues of diplomacy, which now denying and now caressing the most sacred cause and the most solemn rights, makes a mask of them to cover the shame of its object selfishness, what remains there for Italians to do?

Betrayed in their aspirations, and their generous initiative misrepresented, the Treasury overladen with debts, dishonest or incapable men in power, a warlike enemy fortifying himself in the north, with enemies not warlike, but no less iniquitous, who seek to force us to ally ourselves with their frauds or become slaves to their influence, what remains there for Italians to do?

Let them unite; but no longer in support of men whose antecedents of tor-

From *The Times* (London), January 5, 1864, p. 9.

tuous policy promise nought save hatred, discord, renewal of party violence, and fatal disenchantment.

Let them unite; but not in the spirit which by incapacity and malignity has spent the vital forces of the nation in fratricidal conflict.

Let them unite; but in the name of him in whose loyalty alone we confide with filial truth in a supreme crisis—in Victor Emmanuel II.

He alone never failed in his given word. The insidious acts of diplomacy will shiver, as they have ever done, against his truth and honesty. The country may confide in him in the approaching struggle, because he who was ever the bulwark of the destinies of Italy, and who risked his crown in the unequal struggle on the field of battle, will never descend to compromise, but will conduct us gloriously to Rome and Venice.

Let us, then, unite in the name and with the honesty of Victor Emmanuel. Let him be promptly invested with the Dictature of the entire kingdom. Let the Parliament be closed. Let the lists for the conscription open before the arrival of spring for the speedy formation of columns of volunteers, who will form the vanguard of the regular army. Let squadrons of National Guards be formed as a reserve, and let us march without loss of time on the Mincio.

In the name of Italy and Victor Emmanuel Dictator all parties will unite; the brigandage will come which infests the fairest jewel of the Italian crown; the ramparts of Austria will yield; the people of Venice and Myria will rise in insurrection; Italy will regain her own influence, and mistress of her own destinies, will be in a position to seize her capital.

# pierre proudhon

French moralist and advocate of social reform, Pierre Proudhon was born on January 15, 1809, at Besançon, in the Jura mountain district of France. His mother worked as a cook, and his father, who failed in a variety of menial jobs, fought a constant and losing battle against poverty. Although a promising scholar in his youth, Proudhon was forced to leave school in 1827 because of his financial circumstances and he apprenticed himself to a printer; later, as a proof-reader, he acquired knowledge of theology from reading the galley proofs of books and he also taught himself Greek and Hebrew. The revolution of 1830 resulted in economic upheavals, and Proudhon lost his job. He remained un-employed until 1833, when he returned to the printing shop in Besançon. As a recipient of a three year scholarship sponsored by his local municipality to encourage promising young writers, Proudhon was able to attend university lectures in Paris. By 1840 his interests had turned to economics and politics; in that year he published his sensational book *What Is Property?* and answered this question with the resounding reply, "Property is theft."

Proudhon's thinking has been often misrepresented as a socialist attack on private property. Actually his was a defense of property, in that he believed in its equal division among all workers, rather than an attack on the concept of private individual ownership. But the incendiary slogan, appearing as it did when many nations were in the throes of revolution and radical change, brought

Proudhon a kind of notoriety he very likely did not desire. In 1842 his pension was revoked, and he was placed on trial for "offending against religion and morals" but was subsequently acquitted. In 1842 Karl Marx wrote an enthusiastic review of Proudhon's work, but the latter's later publications led Marx bitterly and permanently to break with him. The founder of modern Communism argued that finance capitalism, which Proudhon sought to abolish, and industrial capitalism, which Proudhon wished to strengthen, were inextricably intertwined. This controversy, which was manifest in Proudhon's writing, *The Philosophy of Misery* and in Marx's reply, *The Misery of Philosophy*, is of current interest. It illustrates the roots of the continuing conflict between middle class reformers and the would-be transformers of capitalism.

Proudhon's philosophy is rife with apparent inconsistencies. It is difficult to reconcile his revolutionary sympathies with his sturdy defense of bourgeois family life and his opposition to Italian unification; his egalitarianism with his antifeminism; and his democratic concepts with his opposition to universal suffrage. Although he was a revolutionary, he could not align himself with any revolutionary party. Trotsky called him "the Robinson Crusoe of Socialism." The revolutionary figure with whom Proudhon had the greatest affinity was Bakunin; the aim of revolution, Proudhon insisted, is not a new government, but ultimately no government. He believed that the goal of free society should be anarchy, and that the highest perfection of social organization was that which made the state expendable.

In the revolution of 1848, Proudhon enjoyed an influential position as a recognized leader of radical socialist thought. During June of that year he was elected to the Constituent Assembly, but he soon alienated himself from most of his political allies. His editorial attacks upon the government of Louis Napoleon led to his arrest and trial for sedition in 1849. He was sentenced to three years imprisonment but was permitted to continue editing and writing, and to receive visits from his wife.

Proudhon had married Euphrasie Piegard, a girl from a working class family, while on parole from prison in 1849. Four daughters were born of this union. Upon his release in 1852, Proudhon lived quietly on the outskirts of Paris until 1858 when he published a book which focused upon the fundamental incompatibility of the teaching of the Church and the teaching of the Revolution. The book caused a sensation, particularly in clerical circles, and Proudhon was tried again and sentenced to another three-year term in prison. Before being taken into custody, however, he fled to Belgium and settled in Brussels where he wrote his last important work *La guerre et la paix* (Tolstoy knew the book and may have taken his title for *War and Peace* from it), a peculiar book which both justifies and glorifies war. Proudhon returned to France in 1862 and worked incessantly to support his family by writing. He died at his house at Passy on January 19, 1865, probably of heart failure brought on by asthma. His funeral was attended by a crowd of several thousand.

Much of Proudhon's untrained philosophy is merely perceptive journalism, particularly his treatises on national and international political affairs. But the bulk of his writings had an undeniable impact upon the shaping of French syndicalism. He never surrendered the belief that man's ethical progress would eventually make government unnecessary; and he remained convinced that the abuses of private property were responsible for the most serious injustices in society. Much of his later career was spent in poverty, and the convictions which he expressed in his 1840 study *What Is Property?* did not change in the last twenty-five years of his life. For many, they continue to hold real meaning.

## What Is Property?

If I were asked to answer the following question: *What is slavery?* and I should answer in one word, *It is murder,* my meaning would be understood at once. No extended argument would be required to show that the power to take from a man his thought, his will, his personality, is a power of life and death; and that to enslave a man is to kill him. Why, then, to this other question: *What is property?* may I not likewise answer, *It is robbery* without the certainty of being misunderstood; the second proposition being no other than a transformation of the first?

. . . Such an author teaches that property is a civil right, born of occupation and sanctioned by law; another maintains that it is a natural right, originating in labor,—and both of these doctrines, totally opposed as they may seem, are encouraged and applauded. I contend that neither labor, nor occupation, nor law, can create property; that it is an effect without a cause: am I censurable?

But murmurs arise!

*Property is robbery!* That is the war-cry of 1793! That is the signal of revolutions!

Reader, calm yourself: I am no agent of discord, no firebrand of sedition. I anticipate history by a few days; I disclose a truth whose development we may try in vain to arrest; I write the preamble of our future constitution. This proposition which seems to you blasphemous—*property is robbery*—would, if

From *What Is Property?* The Humboldt Publishing Co., New York, 1890; pp. 11-14, 268-272, 277-282, 284-288.

our prejudices allowed us to consider it, be recognized as the lightning-rod to shield us from the coming thunderbolt; but too many interests stand in the way!...Alas! philosophy will not change the course of events: destiny will fulfill itself regardless of prophecy. Besides, must not justice be done and our education be finished?

*Property is robbery!*... What a revolution in human ideas! *Proprietor* and *robbery* have been at all times expressions as contradictory as the beings whom they designate are hostile; all languages have perpetuated this opposition. On what authority, then do you venture to attack universal consent, and give the lie to the human race? Who are you, that you should question the judgment of the nations and the ages?

Of what consequence to you, reader, is my obscure individuality? I live, like you, in a century in which reason submits only to fact and to evidence. My name, like yours, is TRUTH-SEEKER. My mission is written in these words of the law: *Speak without hatred and without fear; tell that which thou knowest!* The work of our race is to build the temple of science, and this science includes man and Nature. Now, truth reveals itself to all; to-day to Newton and Pascal, to-morrow to the herdsman in the valley and the journeyman in the shop. Each one contributes his stone to the edifice; and, his task accomplished, disappears. Eternity precedes us, eternity follows us; between two infinites, of what account is one poor mortal that the century should inquire about him?

Disregard then, reader, my title and my character, and attend only to my arguments.

...I build no system. I ask an end to privilege, the abolition of slavery, equality of rights, and the reign of law. Justice, nothing else; that is the alpha and omega of my argument: to others I leave the business of governing the world.

One day I asked myself: Why is there so much sorrow and misery in society? Must man always be wretched? And not satisfied with the explanations given by the reformers,—these attributing the general distress to governmental cowardice and incapacity, those to conspirators and *emeutes,* still others to ignorance and general corruption,—and weary of the interminable quarrels of the tribune and the press, I sought to fathom the matter myself.... In this laborious work, I have collected many interesting facts which I shall share with my friends and the public as soon as I have leisure. But I must say that I recognized at once that we had never understood the meaning of these words, so common and yet so sacred: *Justice, equity, liberty;* that concerning each of these principles our ideas have been utterly obscure; and, in fact, that this ignorance was the sole cause both of the poverty that devours us, and of all the calamities that have ever afflicted the human race.

... Justice. .. commences as the right of the strongest. In a society which is trying to organize itself, inequality of faculties calls up the idea of merit; *equit* suggests the plan of proportioning not only esteem, but also material comforts, to personal merit; and since the highest and almost the only merit then recognized is physical strength, the strongest. .. and consequently the best. .. is entitled to the largest share; and if it is refused him, he very naturally takes it by force. From this to the assumption of the right of property in all things, it is but one step.

... From the right of the strongest springs the exploitation of man by man, or bondage; usury, or the tribute levied upon the conquered by the conqueror; and the whole numerous family of taxes, duties, monarchical prerogatives, house-rents, farm-rents, etc.; in one word,—property.

Force was followed by artifice.

... From artifice sprang the profits of manufactures, commerce, and banking, mercantile frauds, and pretensions which are honored with the beautiful names of *talent* and *genius,* but which ought to be regarded as the last degree of knavery and deception; and, finally, all sorts of social inequalities.

In those forms of robbery which are prohibited by law, force and artifice are employed alone and undisguised; in the authorized forms, they conceal themselves within a useful product, which they use as a tool to plunder their victim.

The direct use of violence and strategem was early and universally condemned; but no nation has yet got rid of that kind of robbery which acts through talent, labor, and possession, and which is the source of all the dilemmas of casuistry and the innumerable contradictions of jurisprudence.

The right of force and the right of artifice. .. inspired the legislation of the Greeks and Romans, from which they passed into our morals and codes. Christianity has not changed at all. The Gospel should not be blamed, because the priests, as stupid as the legists, have been unable either to expound or to understand it. The ignorance of councils and popes upon all questions of morality is equal to that of the market-place and the money-changers; and it is this utter ignorance of right, justice, and society, which is killing the Church, and discrediting its teachings for ever. The infidelity of the Roman church and other Christian churches is flagrant; all have disregarded the precept of Jesus; all have erred in moral and doctrinal points; all are guilty of teaching false and absurd dogmas, which lead straight to wickedness and murder. Let it ask pardon of God and men,—this church which called itself infallible, and which has grown so corrupt in morals; let its reformed sisters humble themselves . . . and the people, undeceived, but still religious and merciful, will begin to think.

... The second effect of property is despotism. Now, since despotism is inseparably connected with the idea of legitimate authority, in explaining the natural causes of the first, the principle of the second will appear.

What is to be the form of government in the future? I hear some of my younger readers reply: "Why, how can you ask such a question? You are a republican." "A republican! Yes; but that word specifies nothing. *Res publica;* that is, the public thing. Now, whoever is interested in public affairs—no matter under what form of government—may call himself a republican. Even kings are republicans."—"Well! you are a democrat?"—"No."—"What! you would have a monarchy."—"No."—"A constitutionalist?"—"God forbid!"—"You are then an aristocrat?"—"Not at all."—"You want a mixed government?"—"Still less."—"What are you, then?"—"I am an anarchist."

"Oh! I understand you; you speak satirically. This is a hit at the government."—"By no means. I have just given you my serious and well-considered profession of faith. Although a firm friend of order, I am (in the full force of the term) an anarchist."

... in a given society, the authority of man over man is inversely proportional to the stage of intellectual development which that society has reached; and the probable duration of that authority can be calculated from the more or less general desire for a true government,—that is, for a scientific government. And just as the right of force and the right of artifice retreat before the steady advance of justice, and must finally be extinguished in equality, so the sovereignty of the will yields to the sovereignty of the reason, and must at last be lost in scientific socialism. Property and royalty have been crumbling to pieces ever since the world began. As man seeks justice in equality, so society seeks order in anarchy.

*Anarchy,*—the absence of a master, of a sovereign,—such is the form of government to which we are every day approximating, and which our accustomed habit of taking man for our rule, and his will for law, leads us to regard as the height of disorder and the expression of chaos. The story is told, that a citizen of Paris in the seventeenth century having heard it said that in Venice there was no king, the good man could not recover from his astonishment, and nearly died from laughter at the mere mention of so ridiculous a thing. So strong is our prejudice. As long as we live, we want a chief or chiefs; ... The most advanced among us are those who wish the greatest possible number of sovereigns,—their most ardent wish is for the royalty of the National Guard. Soon, undoubtedly, some one, jealous of the citizen militia, will say, "Everybody is king." But, when he has spoken, I will say, in my turn, "Nobody is king; we are, whether we will or no, associated." Every question of domestic politics must be decided by departmental statistics; every question of foreign politics is an affair of international statistics. The science of government rightly belongs to one of the sections of the Academy of Sciences, whose permanent secretary is necessarily prime minister; and, since every citizen may address a memoir to the Academy, every citizen is a legislator. But, as the opinion of no one is of any value until its truth has been proven, no one can substitute his will for reason,—nobody is king.

. . . I do not see how the liberty of citizens would be endangered by entrusting to their hands, instead of the pen of the legislator, the sword of the law. The executive power, belonging properly to the will, cannot be confided to too many proxies. That is the true sovereignty of the nation.

The proprietor, the robber, the hero, the sovereign—for all these titles are synonymous—imposes his will as law, and suffers neither contradiction nor control; that is, he pretends to be the legislative and the executive power at once. Accordingly, the substitution of the scientific and true law for the royal will is accomplished only by a terrible struggle; and this constant substitution is, after property, the most potent element in history, the most prolific source of political disturbances.

. . . Now, property necessarily engenders despotism,—the government of caprice, the reign of libidinous pleasure. That is so clearly the essence of property that, to be convinced of it, one need but remember what it is, and observe what happens around him. Property is the right to *use* and *abuse*. If, then, government is economy,—if its object is production and consumption, and the distribution of labor and products,—how is government possible while property exists? And if goods are property, why should not the proprietors be kings, and despotic kings. . . . And if each proprietor is sovereign lord within the sphere of his property, absolute king throughout his own domain, how could a government of proprietors be any thing but chaos and confusion?

. . . Then, no government, no public economy, no administration, is possible, which is based upon property.

Communism seeks *equality* and *law*. Property, born of the sovereignty of the reason, and the sense of personal merit, wishes above all things *independence* and *proportionality*.

But communism, mistaking uniformity for law, and levelism for equality, becomes tyrannical and unjust. Property, by its despotism and encroachments, soon proves itself oppressive and anti-social.

The objects of communism and property are good—their results are bad. And why? Because both are exclusive, and each disregards two elements of society. Communism rejects independence and proportionality; property does not satisfy equality and law.

Now, if we imagine a society based upon these four principles,—equality, law, independence, and proportionality,—we find:—

1. That *equality*, consisting only in *equality of condition*, that is, *of means*, and not in *equality of comfort*,—which it is the business of the laborers to achieve for themselves, when provided with equal means,—in no way violates justice and *equit*.

2. That *law*, resulting from the knowledge of facts, and consequently based upon necessity itself, never clashes with independence.

3. That individual *independence*, or the autonomy of the private reason, originating in the difference in talents and capacities, can exist without danger within the limits of the law.

4. That *proportionality*, being admitted only in the sphere of intelligence and sentiment, and not as regards material objects, may be observed without violating justice or social equality.

This third form of society, the synthesis of communism and property, we will call *liberty*.

... Liberty is equality, because liberty exists only in society; and in the absence of equality there is no society.

Liberty is anarchy, because it does not admit the government of the will, but only the authority of the law; that is, of necessity.

Liberty is infinite variety, because it respects all wills within the limits of the law.

Liberty is proportionality, because it allows the utmost latitude to the ambition for merit, and the emulation of glory.

... Liberty is essentially an organizing force. To insure equality between men and peace among nations, agriculture and industry, and the centres of education, business, and storage, must be distributed according to the climate and the geographical position of the country, the nature of the products, the character and natural talents of the inhabitants, etc., in proportions so just, so wise, so harmonious, that in no place shall there ever be either an excess or a lack of population, consumption, and products. There commences the science of public and private right, the true political economy. It is for the writers on jurisprudence, henceforth unembarrassed by the false principle of property, to describe the new laws, and bring peace upon earth. Knowledge and genius they do not lack; the foundation is now laid for them.

I have accomplished my task; property is conquered, never again to arise. Wherever this work is read and discussed, there will be deposited the germ of death to property; there, sooner or later, privilege and servitude will disappear, and the despotism of will will give place to the reign of reason.

... The old civilization has run its race; a new sun is rising, and will soon renew the face of the earth. Let the present generation perish, let the old prevaricators die in the desert! the holy earth shall not cover their bones. Young man, exasperated by the corruption of the age, and absorbed in your zeal for justice!—if your country is dear to you, and if you have the interests of humanity at heart, have the courage to espouse the cause of liberty! Cast off your old selfishness, and plunge into the rising flood of popular equality! There your regenerate soul will acquire new life and vigor; your enervated genius will recover unconquerable energy; and your heart, perhaps already withered, will be rejuvenated! Every thing will wear a different look to your illuminated vision; new sentiments will engender new ideas within you; religion, morality, poetry, art, language will appear before you in nobler and fairer forms; and thenceforth, sure of your faith, and thoughtfully enthusiastic, you will hail the dawn of universal regeneration!

And you, sad victims of an odious law!—you, whom a jesting world despoils and outrages!—you, whose labor has always been fruitless, and whose rest has been without hope,—take courage! your tears are numbered! The fathers have sown in affliction, the children shall reap in rejoicings!

O God of liberty! God of equality! Thou who didst place in my heart the sentiment of justice, before my reason could comprehend it, hear my ardent prayer! Thou hast dictated all that I have written; Thou hast shaped my thought; Thou hast directed my studies; Thou hast weaned my mind from curiosity and my heart from attachment, that I might publish Thy truth to the master and the slave. I have spoken with what force and talent Thou hast given me: it is Thine to finish the work. Thou knowest whether I seek my welfare or Thy glory, O God of liberty! Ah! perish my memory, and let humanity be free! Let me see from my obscurity the people at last instructed; let noble teachers enlighten them; let generous spirits guide them! Abridge, if possible, the time of our trial; stifle pride and avarice in equality; annihilate this love of glory which enslaves us; teach these poor children that in the bosom of liberty there are neither heroes nor great men! Inspire the powerful man, the rich man, him whose name my lips shall never pronounce in Thy presence, with a horror of his crimes; let him be the first to apply for admission to the redeemed society; let the promptness of his repentance be the ground of his forgiveness! Then, great and small, wise and foolish, rich and poor, will unite in an ineffable fraternity; and, singing in unison a new hymn, will rebuild Thy altar, O God of liberty and equality!

# mikhail bakunin

A Russian revolutionary and the most prominent figure among nineteenth century anarchists, Mikhail Bakunin was the eldest son of a retired diplomat and prosperous landowner. Commissioned in 1832, he served for two years with an artillery regiment in eastern Poland before resigning from the military in order to study philosophy. Bakunin left army life because it was dull and regimented, and his interests took him to Berlin university where, for a year and a half, he read Hegel. But Bakunin also rebelled against Hegelian uniformity and concluded that the only true philosophy was the negation of all philosophy; that real religion lay in "political action and the social struggle."

Mikhail Bakunin was by this time a militant atheist whose goals were to spread the religion of revolution and to command personally an international anarchist army. In Paris, he met Karl Marx, whom he criticized for intellectualizing the working classes and thus corrupting their fundamental honesty. He had some contact with the French anarchist Pierre Proudhon, and the latter quite probably influenced his thesis regarding the rise of federal republics, the consequent end of all sovereign states, and the end of the wars endemic to this process. At times he imagined a vast Slavonic federation which would replace the Austrian and Russian empires.

Bakunin played an active role in the Paris rebellion of 1848 and in the Dresden uprising of 1849. Arrested in Dresden on May 10, he was condemned to death.

The sentence was not executed, however, and in 1851 he was turned over to the custody of the Russian government. While serving time in Petropavlovsk prison, Bakunin wrote a formal apologia and confessed to political misdeeds and to fits of madness. Transferred to a penal settlement in eastern Siberia, in 1857, he escaped four years later. By way of Japan and the United States, he reached London, where he began writing for the Russian journal *Kolokol* ("The Bell").

The failure of the Polish rising in 1863 convinced Bakunin to begin in earnest his campaign for universal anarchy. In 1865 he devised a scheme for a global organization, a so-called International Brotherhood of national families secretly manipulated by an international group of coordinators. He condemned the state socialism of Marx as "official democracy and red bureaucracy," and after 1868 he struggled with Marx for control over the First International. Bakunin lost that contest and he later bitterly condemned the Marxists as despots who sought to establish their particular school of thought as the sole source and guide of living. He was also reluctant to place blind faith in the wisdom of the proletariat. Bakunin noted that former manual workers, once they had become rulers and representatives, tended to despise the so-called working class.

When a short-lived commune developed following a rebellion at Lyons in the wake of the Franco-German War of 1870-71, Bakunin rushed to join the insurgents. The revolt failed, as had so many previous efforts in which Bakunin had participated, and he seems ultimately to have lost his old faith in spontaneous popular insurrection as the only sure means of destroying state governments. His influence, nevertheless, remained considerable, and Bakunist "cells" spread from Europe into his native Russia. His followers preached the violent overthrow of the state and embraced Bakunin's view that complete freedom could be achieved through "anarchism, collectivism, and atheism." When he died at Berne, Switzerland, on July 1,1876, Mikhail Bakunin's anarchist revolution seemed an unlikely prospect.

Bakunin's best known work, *God and the State*, was posthumously published in 1882. In his pamphlets and other writings, edited in an English edition by G. P. Maximoff, Bakunin provides his own definitions of the nature and scope of his particular form of social revolution. Like Mao, who warned guerrilla fighters never to alienate the peasants, Bakunin advises the urban proletariat to be cautious in dealing with the rural peasantry. Indeed, he reminds his city followers that a revolution which is imposed upon any class of people is not a revolution at all but rather a form of reactionism. These and other of his considered judgments on revolution follow.

## Scientific Anarchism

Revolutions are not child's play, nor are they academic debates in which only, vanities are hurt in furious clashes, nor literary jousts wherein only ink is spilled profusely. Revolution means war, and that implies the destruction of men and things. Of course it is a pity that humanity has not yet invented a more peaceful means of progress, but until now every forward step in history has been achieved only after it has been baptized in blood. For that matter, reaction can hardly reproach revolution on this point; it has always shed more blood than the latter.

Revolution is overthrow of the State.

... Every political revolution which does not have economic equality as its *immediate* and *direct* aim is, from the point of view of popular interests and rights, only a hypocritical and disguised reaction.

According to the almost unanimous opinion of the German Socialists, *a political revolution has to precede a social revolution*—which, in my opinion, is a grave and fatal error, because every political revolution which takes place prior to and consequently apart from a social revolution, necessarily will be a bourgeois revolution, and a bourgeois revolution can only further bourgeois Socialism; that is, it will necessarily end in new exploitation of the proletariat by the bourgeoisie—exploitation perhaps more skilful and hypocritical, but certainly no less oppressive.

... Either the bourgeois-educated world will subdue and then enslave the rebellious, elemental forces of the people in order, through the power of the knout and bayonets (consecrated, of course, by some sort of divinity and rationalized by science), to force the working masses to toil as they have been doing, which leads directly to re-establishment of the State in its most natural form, that is, the form of a military dictatorship or rule by an Emperor—or the working masses will throw off the hateful, age-long yoke, and will destroy to its very roots bourgeois exploitation and bourgeois civilization based upon that exploitation; and that would mean the triumph of the Social Revolution, the uprooting of all that is represented by the State.

Thus the State, on the one hand, and social revolution, on the other hand, are the two opposite poles, the antagonism which constitutes the very essence of the genuine social life of the whole continent of Europe.

... The Social Revolution must put an end to the old system of organization based upon violence, giving full liberty to the masses, groups, communes, and associations, and likewise to individuals themselves, and destroying once and for all the historic cause of all violences, the power and the very existence of the

From *The Political Philosophy of Bakunin: Scientific Anarchism*, edited by G. P. Maximoff, The Free Press, Glencoe, Illinois, 1953, pp. 372-379, 397-404, 407-408, 413-415.

State, the downfall of which will carry down with it all the iniquities of juridical right, and all the falsehoods of the diverse religious cults—that right and those cults being simply the complaisant consecration (ideal as well as real) of all the violences represented, guaranteed, and furthered by the State.

Within the depths of the proletariat itself—at first within the French and Austrian proletariat, and then in that of the rest of Europe—there began to crystallize and finally took shape an altogether new tendency which aims directly at sweeping away every form of exploitation and every kind of political and juridical as well as governmental oppression—that is, at the abolition of all classes by means of economic equality and the abolition of their last bulwark, the State.

Such is the program of the Social Revolution.

Thus at present there exists in all the civilized countries in the world only one universal problem—the fullest and final emancipation of the proletariat from economic exploitation and State oppression. It is clear then that this question cannot be solved without a terrible and bloody struggle, and that in view of that situation the right and the importance of every nation will depend upon the direction, character, and degree of its participation in this struggle.

. . . But social revolution cannot be confined to a single people: it is international in its very essence.

Under the historic, juridical, religious, and social organization of most civilized countries, the economic emancipation of the workers is a sheer impossibility—and consequently, in order to attain and fully carry out that emancipation, it is necessary to destroy all modern institutions: the State, Church, Courts, University, Army, and Police, all of which are ramparts erected by the privileged classes against the proletariat. And it is not enough to have them overthrown in one country only: it is essential to have them destroyed in all countries, for since the emergence of modern States—in the seventeenth and eighteenth centuries—there has existed among those countries and those institutions an ever-growing international solidarity and powerful international alliances.

. . . Revolutions are not improvised. They are not made at will by individuals, and not even by the most powerful associations. They come about through force of circumstances, and are independent of any deliberate will or conspiracy. They can be foreseen. . . but never can their explosion be accelerated.

. . . The time of great political personalities is over. When it was a question of waging political revolutions, those individuals were in their place. Politics has for its object the foundation and preservation of the States; but he who says "the State" says domination on one hand and subjection on the other. Great dominant individuals are absolutely necessary in a political revolution; in a social revolution they are not only useless, they are positively harmful and are incompatible with the foremost aim of that revolution, the emancipation of the masses. At present, in revolutionary action as in modern labor, the collective must supplant the individual.

In a social revolution, which is diametrically opposed in every way to a political revolution, the actions of individuals are virtually null while the spontaneous action of the masses should be everything. All that individuals can do is to elaborate, clarify, and propagate ideas corresponding to the popular instinct and contribute their incessant efforts to the revolutionary organization of the natural power of the masses, but nothing over and above that; the rest can and should be done by the masses themselves.

... As to organization, it is necessary in order that when the Revolution, brought about through the force of circumstances, breaks out in full power, there be a real force in the field, one that knows what should be done and by virtue thereof capable of taking hold of the Revolution and giving it a direction salutary for the people: a serious international organization of workers' associations in all countries, capable of replacing the departing political world of the States and the bourgeoisie.

Universal public and private bankruptcy is the first condition for a social-economic revolution.

... But States do not crumble by themselves; they are overthrown by a universal international social organization. And organizing popular forces to carry out that revolution—such is the only task of those who sincerely aim at emancipation.

... The initiative in the new movement will belong to the people ... in Western Europe, to the city and factory workers—in Russia, Poland, and most of the Slavic countries, to the peasants.

But in order that the peasants rise up, it is absolutely necessary that the initiative in this revolutionary movement be taken by the city workers, for it is the latter who combine in themselves the instincts, ideas, and conscious will of the Social Revolution. Consequently, the whole danger threatening the existence of the States is focused in the city proletariat.

... The social transformation to which we wholeheartedly aspire is the great act of justice, finding its basis in the rational organization of society with equal rights for all.

... Even profound historians and jurists have not understood the simple truth, the explanation and confirmation of which they could have read on every page of history, namely: that in order to render harmless any political force whatever, to pacify and subdue it, only one way is possible, and that is to proceed with its destruction. Philosophers have not understood that against political forces there can be no other guarantees but complete destruction; that in politics, as in the arena of mutually struggling forces and facts, words, promises, and vows mean nothing—and that is so because every political force, while it remains an actual force, even apart from and contrary to the will of the kings and other authorities who direct it, must steadfastly tend toward the realization of its own aims; this by virtue of its essential nature and because of the danger of self-destruction.

... And be on guard—a question reduced to terms of force remains a doubtful question.

But if force cannot obtain justice for the proletariat, what is capable of obtaining it? A miracle? We do not believe in miracles, and those who speak to the proletariat of such miracles are liars and corrupters. Moral propaganda? The moral conversion of the bourgeoisie under the influence of Mazzini's sermons? But it is utterly wrong on the part of Mazzini, who certainly should know history, to speak of such a conversion and to lull the proletariat with those ridiculous illusions. Was there ever, at any period, or in any country, a single example of a privileged and dominant class which granted concessions freely, spontaneously, and without being driven to it by force or fear?

... The awareness of the justice of its own cause is no doubt vital to the proletariat in order to organize its own members into a power capable of attaining a triumph. And the proletariat now does not lack this awareness. Where such awareness is still lacking it is our duty to build it up among the workers; that justice has become incontestable even in the eyes of our adversaries. But the mere consciousness of such justice is not sufficient. It is necessary that the proletariat add to it the organization of its own forces, for the time is passed when the walls of Jericho would crumble at the blowing of trumpets; now force is necessary to vanquish and repulse other force.

... We say to the workers: The justice of your cause is certain; only scoundrels can deny it. What you lack, however, is the organization of your own forces. Organize those forces and overthrow that which stands in the way of the realization of your justice. Begin by striking down all those who oppress you. And then after having assured your victory and having destroyed the power of your enemies, show yourselves humane toward the unfortunate stricken-down foes, henceforth disarmed and harmless; recognize them as your brothers and invite them to live and work alongside of you upon the unshakable foundation of social equality.

... Fortunately the proletariat of the cities, not excepting those who swear by the names of Mazzini and Garibaldi, never could let itself be completely converted to the ideas and cause of Mazzini and Garibaldi. And the workers could not do it for the simple reason that the proletariat—that is, the oppressed, despoiled, maltreated, miserable, starved mass of workers—necessarily possess the logic inherent in the historic role of labor.

Workers may accept the programs of Mazzini and Garibaldi; but deep down in their bellies, in the livid pallor of their children and their companions in poverty and suffering, in their everyday actual slavery, there is something which calls for a social revolution. They are all Socialists in spite of themselves, with the exception of a few individuals—perhaps one out of thousands—who, owing to a certain cleverness, to chance or knavery on their part, have entered, or hope to enter, the ranks of the bourgeoisie. All others—and I am referring to the masses of workers who follow Mazzini and Garibaldi—are such only in their imagination, and in reality they can be only revolutionary Socialists.

. . . If you will organize yourselves for this purpose throughout Italy, harmoniously, fraternally, without recognizing any leaders but your own young collective, I vow to you that within the year there will be no more Mazzinist or Garibaldist workers; they all will be revolutionary Socialists, and patriots, too, but in a very human sense of that word. That is, they will simultaneously be both patriots and internationalists. Thus you will create an unshakable foundation for the future of the Social Revolution.

. . . Organize the city proletariat in the name of revolutionary Socialism, and in doing this, unite it into one preparatory organization together with the peasantry. An uprising by the proletariat alone would not be enough; with that we would have only a political revolution which would necessarily produce a natural and legitimate reaction on the part of the peasants, and that reaction, or merely the indifference of the peasants, would strangle the revolution of the cities, as it happened recently in France.

Only a wide-sweeping revolution embracing both the city workers and peasants would be sufficiently strong to overthrow and break the organized power of the State, backed as it is by all the resources of the possessing classes. But an all-embracing revolution, that is, a social revolution, is a simultaneous revolution of the people of the cities and of the peasantry. It is this kind of revolution that must be organized—for without a preparatory organization, the most powerful elements are insignificant and impotent. . . .

The principal reason why all the revolutionary authorities in the world have accomplished so little toward the Revolution *is that they always wanted to create the Revolution themselves, by their own authority and by their own power*, a circumstance which never failed to produce two results:

In the first place, it greatly narrowed down revolutionary activity, for it is impossible even for the most intelligent, most energetic, most candid revolutionary authority to encompass at once the great number of questions and interests stirred up by the Revolution. For every dictatorship (individual as well as collective, in so far as it is made up of several official persons) is necessarily very circumscribed, very blind, and is incapable of either penetrating the depths or comprehending the scope of the people's lives, just as it is impossible for the largest and most powerful sea-going vessel to measure the depth and expanse of the ocean. Second, every act of official authority, legally imposed, necessarily awakens within the masses a rebellious feeling, a legitimate counter-reaction.

What should revolutionary authorities—and let us try to have as few of them as possible—do in order to organize the Revolution? *They must not do it themselves, by revolutionary decrees, by imposing this task upon the masses; rather their aim should be that of provoking the masses to action. They must not try to impose upon the masses any organization whatever, but rather should induce the people to set up autonomous organizations. This can be done by gaining influence over the most intelligent and advanced individuals of high standing in each locality*, so that these organizations will conform as much as possible to our principles. Therein lies the whole secret of our triumph.

... There is no need to grumble nor to scorn or disparage the peasants. *It is necessary to lay down a line of revolutionary conduct which will obviate the difficulty of proselytizing the peasants and which will not only prevent the individualism of the peasants from pushing them into the camp of reaction but, on the contrary, will make it instrumental in the triumph of the Revolution.*

Remember, my dear friends, and keep repeating to yourselves a hundred, a thousand times a day, that upon the establishment of this line of conduct depends the outcome of the Revolution: victory or defeat.

... I do not believe that even under the most favorable circumstances the city workers will have sufficient power to impose Communism or collectivism upon the peasants; and I have never wanted this way of realizing Socialism, because I hate every system imposed by force, and because I sincerely and passionately love freedom. This false idea and this hope are destructive of liberty and they constitute the basic delusion of authoritarian Communism, which, because it needs the regularly organized violence of the State, and thus needs the State, necessarily leads to the re-establishment of the principle of authority and of a privileged class of the State.

Collectivism can be imposed only upon slaves—and then collectivism becomes the negation of humanity. Among a free people collectivism can come about only in the natural course of things, by force of circumstances, not by imposing it from above, but by a spontaneous movement from below, which springs forth freely and necessarily when the conditions of privileged individualism—State politics, the codes of civil and criminal law, the juridical family and inheritance rights—have been swept away by the Revolution.

... One must be mad, I have said, to impose anything upon the peasants under present conditions: it would surely make enemies out of them and surely would ruin the Revolution. What are the principal grievances of the peasants, the main causes of their sullen and deep hatred for the cities?

1. The peasants feel that the cities despise them, and that contempt is felt directly, even by the children, and is never forgiven.

2. The peasants imagine, *not without plenty of reasons,* although lacking sufficient historic proofs and experiences to back up those assumptions, that the cities want to dominate and govern them, that they frequently want to exploit them, and that they always want to impose upon the peasants a political order which is very little to the liking of the latter.

3. In addition, the peasants consider the city workers *partisans of dividing up property,* and they fear that the Socialists will confiscate their land, which they love above everything else.

... Then what should the city workers do in order to overcome this distrust and enmity of the peasants toward themselves? In the first place, they must cease displaying their contempt, stop despising the peasants. This is necessary for the salvation of the Revolution and of the workers themselves, for the hatred of the peasants constitutes an immense danger. Had it not been for this distrust and hatred, the Revolution would long ago have become an accomplished fact, for it is this animosity, which unfortunately the peasants have been showing toward the cities, that in all countries serves as the basis and the principal force of reaction. In the interest of the revolution which is to emancipate the industrial workers, the latter must get rid of their supercilious attitude toward the peasants. They also should do this for the sake of justice, for in reality they have no reason to despise or detest the peasants. The peasants are not idling parasites, they are rugged workers like the city proletariat. Only they toil under different conditions. In the presence of bourgeois exploitation, the city workers should feel themselves brothers of the peasants.

... The peasants will join cause with the city workers as soon as they become convinced that the latter do not pretend to impose upon them their will or some political and social order invented by the cities for the greater happiness of the villages; they will join cause as soon as they are assured that the industrial workers will not take their lands away.

It is altogether necessary at the present moment that the city workers really renounce this claim and this intention, and that they renounce it in such a manner that the peasants get to know and become convinced of it. Those workers must renounce it, for even when that claim and that intention seemed to lie within the bounds of realization, they were *highly unjust and reactionary,* and now when that realization becomes impossible, it would be no less than criminal folly to attempt it.

By what right would the city workers impose upon the peasants any form of government or economic organization whatever? By the right of revolution, we are told. But the Revolution ceases to be a revolution when it acts despotically, when, instead of promoting freedom among the masses, it promotes reaction. The means and condition, if not the principal aim of the Revolution, is the annihilation of the principle of authority in all of its possible manifestations—the abolition, the utter destruction, and, if necessary, the violent destruction of the State. For the State, the lesser brother of the Church, as Proudhon has proven it, is the historic consecration of all despotisms, of all privileges, the political reason for all economic and social enslavement, the very essence and focal point of all reaction. Therefore, whenever a State is built up in the name of the Revolution, it is reaction and despotism that are being furthered and not freedom, it is the establishment of privilege versus equality that comes as a result thereof.

... This is as clear as daylight. But the Socialist workers of France, brought up in the political traditions of Jacobinism, have never wanted to understand it. Now they will be compelled to understand it, which is fortunate for the Revolution and for themselves. Whence this ridiculous as well as arrogant, unjust as well as baneful, claim on their part to impose their political and social ideal upon ten million peasants who do not want it? Manifestly this is one more bourgeois legacy, a political bequest of bourgeois revolutionism. What is the basis, the explanation, the underlying theory of this claim? It is the pretended or real superiority of intelligence, of education—in a word, of workers' civilization over that of the rural population.

But do you realize that with this principle one could easily justify any kind of conquest and oppression? The bourgeoisie have always fallen back upon that principle to prove their mission and their right to *govern* or, what amounts to the same thing, to exploit the world of labor. In conflicts between nations as well as between classes this fatal principle, which is simply the principle of authority, explains and poses as a right all invasions and conquests. Did not the Germans always put forth this principle by way of justifying their attempts upon the liberty and independence of the Slavic peoples and of legitimizing the violent and forcible Germanization of the latter? That, they say, is the victory of civilization over barbarism.

Beware, the Germans already are remarking that the German Protestant civilization is much superior to the Catholic civilization of the peoples of the Latin race in general, and of the French civilization in particular. Beware lest the Germans soon imagine that their mission is to civilize you and to make you happy, just as you now imagine that it is your mission to civilize and forcibly free your compatriots, your brothers, the peasants of France. To me both claims are equally hateful, and I declare to you that in international relations, as well as in the relations of one class to another, I will be on the side of those who are to be civilized in this manner. Together with them I will revolt against all those arrogant civilizers—whether they call themselves Germans or workers—and in rebelling against them I shall serve the cause of revolution against reaction.

... But if this is the case, I shall be asked, must we then abandon the ignorant and superstitious peasants to all kinds of influences and intrigues, on the part of reaction? Not at all! Reaction must be destroyed in the villages just as it has to be destroyed in the cities. But in order to attain this goal, it is not enough to say: We want to destroy reaction; it must be destroyed and torn out by its roots, which can be done only by decrees. On the contrary—and I can prove it by citing history—decrees, and in general all acts of authority extirpate nothing; they perpetuate that which they set out to destroy.

What follows? Since revolution cannot be *imposed* upon the villages, *it must be generated right there, by promoting a revolutionary movement among the peasants themselves, leading them on to destroy through their own efforts the public order, all the political and civil institutions, and to establish and organize anarchy in the villages.*

But what is to be done? There is only one way—and that is, to revolutionize the villages as much as the cities. But who can do it? The only class which is now the real outspoken agent of the Revolution is the working class of the cities.

... *It is necessary to send free detachments into the villages as propagandists for the Revolution.*

There is a general rule to the effect that those who want to spread the Revolution by means of propaganda must be revolutionists themselves. One must have the Devil within himself in order to be able to arouse the masses; otherwise there can be only abortive speeches and empty clamor, but not revolutionary acts. Therefore, above all else the propagandistic free detachments have to be inspired and organized along revolutionary lines. They must carry the Revolution within themselves in order to be able to provoke and arouse it in their listeners. And then they have to draw up a plan, a line of conduct conforming to the aim which they have set for themselves.

What is this aim? It is not to impose the Revolution upon the peasants, but to provoke and arouse it among them. A revolution that is imposed upon people—whether by official decree or by force of arms—is not a revolution, but its opposite, for it necessarily provokes reaction.

... Civil war, so baneful for the power of the States, is on the contrary and by virtue of this very cause, always favorable to the awakening of popular initiative and the intellectual, moral, and even material development of the people. The reason thereof is quite simple: civil war upsets and disturbs in the masses the sheepish state so beloved of all governments, a state turning the people into herds to be tended and to be shorn at will by their shepherds. Civil war breaks up the brutalizing monotony of their daily existence, a mechanical existence devoid of thought, and compels them to reflect upon the claims of the various princes or parties contending for the right to oppress and exploit the masses of people. And it often leads them to the realization—if not conscious at least instinctive realization—of the profound truth that neither one of the contending parties has any claim upon them, and that both are equally bad.

Besides, from the moment that the people's collective mind, which is usually kept in a state of torpor, wakes up at one point, it necessarily asserts itself in other directions. It becomes stirred up, it breaks away from its worldly inertia, and, transcending the confines of a mechanical faith, shaking off the yoke of traditional and petrified representations which have served it in the place of genuine thoughts, it subjects all its idols of yesterday to a passionate and severe criticism, one that is guided by its own sound sense and upright conscience, which often are of greater value than science.

It is thus that the people's mind awakens. And with the awakening of that mind comes the sacred instinct, the essentially human instinct of revolt, the source of all emancipation; and simultaneously there develop within the people morality and material prosperity—those twin children of freedom. This freedom, so beneficial to the people, finds its support, guarantee, and encouragement in the civil war itself, which, by dividing the forces of the people's oppressors, exploiters, tutors, and masters, necessarily undermines the baneful power of one and the other.

. . . All the other classes [except the city and rural proletariat] must vanish from the face of the earth; they must vanish not as individuals but as classes. Socialism is not cruel; it is a thousand times more humane than Jacobinism, that is, than the political revolution. It is not directed against individuals, not even against the most nefarious among them, since it realizes only too well that all individuals, good or bad, are the inevitable product of the social status created for them by society and history. True, Socialists will not be able to prevent the people in the early days of the Revolution from giving vent to their fury by doing away with a few hundreds of the most odious, the most rabid and dangerous enemies. But once that hurricane passes, the Socialists will oppose with all their might hypocritical—in a political and juridical sense—butchery perpetrated in cold blood.

. . . As soon as the Revolution begins to take on a Socialist character, it will cease to be cruel and sanguinary. The people are not at all cruel; it is the ruling classes that have shown themselves to be cruel. At times the people rise up, raging against all the deceits, vexations, oppressions, and tortures, of which they are victims, and then they break forth like an enraged bull, seeing nothing ahead of them and demolishing everything in their way. But those are very rare and very brief moments. Ordinarily the people are good and humane. They suffer too much themselves not to sympathize with the sufferings of others.

But alas! too often have they served as instruments of the systematic fury of the privileged classes. All the national, political, and religious ideas, for the sake of which the people have shed their own blood and the blood of their brothers, the blood of foreign peoples, all these ideas have always served only the interests of those classes, ever turning into means of new oppression and exploitation of the people. In all the furious scenes in the history of all the countries wherein the masses of the people, enraged to the point of madness, have turned their energies to mutual destruction, you will invariably find that behind those masses are agitators and leaders belonging to the privileged classes: Army officers, noblemen, priests, and bourgeois. It is not among the people that one should look for cruelty and concentrated and systematically organized cold fury, but in the instincts, the passions, and the political and religious institutions of the privileged classes: in the Church and in the State, in their laws, and in the ruthless and iniquitous application of those laws.

. . . It inevitably comes about that after killing many people, the revolutionaries see themselves driven to the melancholy conviction that nothing has been gained and that not a single step has been made toward the realization of their cause, but that, on the contrary, they did an ill turn to the Revolution by employing those methods, and that they prepared with their own hands the triumph of reaction. And that is so for two reasons: first, that the causes of the reaction having been left intact, the reaction is given a chance to reproduce and multiply itself in new forms; and second, that ere long all those bloody butcheries and massacres must arouse against them everything that is human in man.

The [French] revolution . . . whatever one may say about it, was neither Socialist nor materialist, nor, using the pretentious expression of M. Gambetta, was it by any means a *positivist* revolution. It was essentially bourgeois, Jacobin, metaphysical, political, and idealist. Generous and sweeping in its aspirations, it reached out for an impossible thing: establishment of an ideal equality in the midst of material inequality. While preserving as *sacred foundations* all the conditions of economic inequality, it believed that it could unite and envelop all men in a sweeping sentiment of brotherly, humane, intellectual, moral, political, and social equality. That was its dream, its religion, manifested by the enthusiasm, by the grandly heroic acts of its best and greatest representatives. But the realization of that dream was impossible because it ran contrary to all natural and social laws.

# karl marx

Karl Marx, German political philosopher and the most important figure in the history of socialist thinking, was born in Trier, the son of an enlightened and successful lawyer. Although both his father and his Dutch mother were descendants of Jewish rabbinical families, Marx's father had converted to Lutheranism and all members of the family were baptized Protestants. Consequently, Marx never held any particular racial, religious, or national allegiance but always considered himself a European.

During his student days at the universities of Bonn and Berlin, young Karl distinguished himself as an excellent student in law, political science, philosophy, and history. After receiving his doctoral degree in philosophy in 1842 from the University of Jena, Marx's liberal political views led him to consider journalism as a career. In 1842 he became editor of the *Rheinische Zeitung*, a liberal newspaper in Cologne.

Marx married Jenny von Westphalen in 1843. Also the product of a bourgeois background, Jenny was the daughter of a high government official and had been a close friend from the days of Karl's boyhood. Their marriage was a happy one, although the tribulations of subsequent years occasionally contributed to some severe strain. Six children were born of this union; only three survived childhood. When Marx's newspaper was suppressed by the government in 1843, he and Jenny moved to Paris where they met a wealthy manufacturer's son, Friedrich Engels, who became a lifelong friend, collaborator, and supporter.

In 1847, at a new place of exile in Brussels, Marx wrote a reply to Pierre Proudhon's book *The Philosophy of Misery* and entitled it *The Misery of Philosophy*. In this work he developed the fundamental propositions of his economic interpretation of history. His opposition to utopian socialists like Proudhon derived from his distrust of any scheme which sought the morally most desirable order. Marx's early Hegelian training had rendered him a determinist, and he believed that the system which soon would replace capitalism would by necessity emerge from the inevitable operation of historical forces. It was also during his stay in Brussels that Marx, who was gaining increasing prominence in socialist circles, was commissioned by the London Center of the Communist League to compose a definite statement of its aims and beliefs. This work appeared as *Manifest der Kommunistischen Partei* ("Manifesto of the Communist Party"). Published in 1848, it is a historic document of tremendous force, succinctness, and clarity which has achieved worldwide significance.

The revolutionary atmosphere in Germany in 1848 enabled Marx to return to Cologne and revive his newspaper under the title of *Neue Rheinische Zeitung,* but in 1849 he was expelled. This time he settled in London, where he spent the rest of his life in poverty. The generosity of his friend and benefactor Engels, and the income earned from commissioned writings for such newspapers as the *New York Tribune,* then under the editorship of a utopian socialist, spared Marx from starvation. Several of Marx's children died, among them Edgar, the only son from his marriage. He also had an illegitimate son, Frederic, about whom little is known. Of Marx's three daughters who reached adulthood, two married French socialists; the third committed suicide after an unhappy association with British Marxist Edward Aveling. Marx died on March 14, 1883, fifteen months after the death of his wife. He was buried at Highgate cemetery in London.

Despite poverty and persistent illness, Marx was a prolific writer. He published numerous articles and books, but his most famous work was *Das Kapital.* The first volume appeared in 1867; the second and third volumes, published posthumously in 1885 and 1894, were edited by Engels. Collectively, these volumes provide a thorough exposition of Marxism and they became the foundation of international socialism. As Marx's reputation spread, so did public fear of him. He had insisted on authoritarian sway within the International, and finally, after controversy with Bakunin, virtually destroyed the International rather than risk losing control over its direction.

Marx was primarily a revolutionist who was interested in ideas only as a means of influencing the course of events. Convinced of the righteousness of his cause, he was intolerant of criticism and contradiction. His was a powerful, incisive, unsentimental, and thoroughly practical mind. Marx's method was developed according to practical intellectual principles which considered the feasibility of achievement. He termed himself a "scientific" socialist in contradistinction to the utopian socialists. Regarding Czarist Russia as the greatest enemy of freedom in all Europe, Marx wished to see British imperial power bolstered as a counter-weight. He also hated the autocratic rule of Napoleon III and Bismarck. Occasionally he was capable of sharing national feelings, exemplified in his passionate interest in the American Civil War and championing of the North. Since Marx treasured the liberal-humanitarian tradition from which the socialist movement had sprung, he very probably would abhor the antihumanitarian practices of some contemporary Communist regimes.

Marx's purpose was to provide a social philosophy for the rising proletariat. Although he regarded the course of history as proceeding from timeless economic laws toward the predetermined goal of socialism, he felt a mission to accelerate this inevitable historical process. To Marx, private ownership was the source of all evil in society; it produced class distinctions, class interests, and ultimately, class struggle. As he stated in his *Manifesto of the Communist Party* (selections from which follow), "The history of all hitherto existing society is the history of class struggles." The importance of his dialectical method and of his theories extends far beyond their immense political influence. Estimates of Marx vary greatly. Communists look to him as their messiah; countless scholars consider him the founder of economic history and sociology; some regard him as an unscrupulous, bloodthirsty destroyer of society. In general, however, Marx should be viewed against the background of the early industrial society whose injustices he so effectively attacked. In his book entitled *Karl Marx,* Isaiah Berlin states: "No thinker in the nineteenth century has had so direct, deliberate and powerful an influence upon mankind as Karl Marx." Only the future will tell whether his legacy will have equal import for this and subsequent centuries.

## Manifesto of the Communist Party

... The history of all hitherto existing society is the history of class struggles.

Freeman and slave, patrician and plebeian, lord and serf, guild-master and journeyman, in a word, oppressor and oppressed, stood in constant opposition

From *Karl Marx and Friedrich Engels: Selected Works,* I, Foreign Languages Publishing House, Moscow, 1955, pp. 34-49, 51-54, 64-65.

to one another, carried on an uninterrupted, now hidden, now open fight, a fight that each time ended, either in a revolutionary re-constitution of society at large, or in the common ruin of the contending classes.

... The modern bourgeois society that has sprouted from the ruins of feudal society has not done away with class antagonisms. It has but established new classes, new conditions of oppression, new forms of struggle in place of the old ones.

Our epoch, the epoch of the bourgeoisie, possesse, however, this distinctive feature: it has simplified the class antagonisms. Society as a whole is more and more splitting up into two great hostile camps, into two great classes directly facing each other: Bourgeoisie and Proletariat.

... The bourgeoisie, historically, has played a most revolutionary part.

The bourgeoisie, wherever it has got the upper hand, has put an end to all feudal, patriarchal, idyllic relations. It has pitilessly torn asunder the motley feudal ties that bound man to his "natural superiors," and has left remaining no other nexus between man and man than naked self-interest, then callous "cash payment." It has drowned the most heavenly ecstasies of religious fervour, of chivalrous enthusiasm, of philistine sentimentalism, in the icy water of egotistical calculation. It has resolved personal worth into exchange value, and in place of the numberless indefeasible chartered freedoms, has set up that single, unconscionable freedom—Free Trade. In one word, for exploitation, veiled by religious and political illusions, it has substituted naked, shameless, direct, brutal exploitation.

... The bourgeoisie has subjected the country to the rule of the towns. It has created enormous cities, has greatly increased the urban population as compared with the rural, and has thus rescued a considerable part of the population from the idiocy of rural life. Just as it has made the country dependent on the towns, so it has made barbarian and semi-barbarian countries dependent on the civilized ones, nations of peasants on nations of bourgeois, the East on the West.

The bourgeoisie keeps more and more doing away with the scattered state of the population, of the means of production, and of property. It has agglomerated population, centralized means of production, and has concentrated property in a few hands. The necessary consequence of this was political centralization. Independent, or but loosely connected provinces, with separate interests, laws, governments and systems of taxation, became lumped together into one nation, with one government, one code of laws, one national class-interest, one frontier and one customs-tariff.

... Modern bourgeois society with its relations of production, of exchange and of property, a society that has conjured up such gigantic means of production and of exchange, is like the sorcerer, who is no longer able to control the powers of the nether world whom he has called up by his spells. For many a decade past the history of industry and commerce is but the history of the revolt of modern productive forces against modern conditions of production, against the property relations that are the conditions for the existence of the bourgeoisie and of its rule. It is enough to mention the commercial crises that by their periodical return put on its trial, each time more threateningly, the existence of the entire bourgeois society. In these crises a great part not only of the existing products, but also of the previously created productive forces, are periodically destroyed. In these crises there breaks out an epidemic that, in all earlier epochs, would have seemed an absurdity—the epidemic of overproduction. Society suddenly finds itself put back into a state of momentary barbarism; it appears as if a famine, a universal war of devastation had cut off the supply of every means of subsistence; industry and commerce seem to be destroyed: and why? Because there is too much civilisation, too much means of subsistence, too much industry, too much commerce. The productive forces at the disposal of society no longer tend to further the development of the conditions of bourgeois property; on the contrary, they have become too powerful for these conditions, by which they are fettered, and so soon as they overcome these fetters, they bring disorder into the whole of bourgeois society, endanger the existence of bourgeois property. The conditions of bourgeois society are too narrow to comprise the wealth created by them. And how does the bourgeoisie get over these crises? On the one hand by enforced destruction of a mass of productive forces; on the other, by the conquest of new markets, and by the more thorough exploitation of the old ones. That is to say, by paving the way for more extensive and more destructive crises, and by diminishing the means whereby crises are prevented.

The weapons with which the bourgeoisie felled feudalism to the ground are now turned against the bourgeoisie itself.

But not only has the bourgeoisie forged the weapons that bring death to itself; it has also called into existence the men who are to wield those weapons—the modern working class—the proletarians.

In proportion as the bourgeoisie, i.e., capital, is developed, in the same proportion is the proletariat, the modern working class, developed—a class of labourers, who live only so long as they find work, and who find work only so long as their labour increases capital. These labourers, who must sell themselves piecemeal, are a commodity, like every other article of commerce, and are consequently exposed to all the vicissitudes of competition, to all the fluctuations of the market.

... Modern industry has converted the little workshop of the patriarchal master into the great factory of the industrial capitalist. Masses of labourers, crowded into the factory, are organised like soldiers. As privates of the industrial army they are placed under the command of a perfect hierarchy of officers and sergeants. Not only are they slaves of the bourgeois class, and of the bourgeois State; they are daily and hourly enslaved by the machine, by the over-looker, and, above all, by the individual bourgeois manufacturer himself. The more openly this despotism proclaims gain to be its end and aim, the more petty, the more hateful and the more embittering it is.

. . . with the development of industry the proletariat not only increases in number; it becomes concentrated in greater masses, its strength grows, and it feels that strength more. The various interests and conditions of life within the ranks of the proletariat are more and more equalised, in proportion as machinery obliterates all distinctions of labour, and nearly everywhere reduces wages to the same low level. The growing competition among the bourgeois, and the resulting commercial crises, make the wages of the workers ever more fluctuating. The unceasing improvement of machinery, ever more rapidly developing, makes their livelihood more and more precarious; the collisions between individual workmen and individual bourgeois take more and more the character of collisions between two classes. Thereupon the workers begin to form combinations (Trades' Unions) against the bourgeois; they club together in order to keep up the rate of wages; they found permanent associations in order to make provision beforehand for these occasional revolts. Here and there the contest breaks out into riots.

. . . .This organization of the proletarians into a class, and consequently into a political party, is continually being upset again by the competition between the workers themselves. But it ever rises up again, stronger, firmer, mightier. It compels legislative recognition of particular interests of the workers, by taking advantage of the divisions among the bourgeoisie itself.

. . . .Of all the classes that stand face to face with the bourgeoisie today, the proletariat alone is a really revolutionary class. The other classes decay and finally disappear in the face of modern industry; the proletariat is its special and essential product.

. . . .The proletarians cannot become masters of the productive forces of society, except by abolishing their own previous mode of appropriation, and thereby also every other previous mode of appropriation. They have nothing of their own to secure and to fortify; their mission is to destroy all previous securities for, and insurances of, individual property.

All previous historical movements were movements of minorities, or in the interest of minorities. The proletarian movement is the self-conscious, independent movement of the immense majority, in the interests of the immense majority. The proletariat, the lowest stratum of our present society, cannot stir, cannot raise itself up, without the whole superincumbent strata of official society being sprung into the air.

Though not in substance, yet in form, the struggle of the proletariat with the bourgeoisie is at first a national struggle. The proletariat of each country must, of course, first of all settle matters with its own bourgeoisie.

In depicting the most general phases of the development of the proletariat, we traced the more or less veiled civil war, raging within existing society, up to the point where that war breaks out into open revolution, and where the violent overthrow of the bourgeoisie lays the foundation for the sway of the proletariat.

. . . .The essential condition for the existence, and for the sway of the bourgeois class, is the formation and augmentation of capital; the condition for capital is wage-labour. Wage-labour rests exclusively on competition between the labourers. The advance of industry, whose involuntary promoter is the bourgeoisie, replaces the isolation of the labourers, due to competition, by their revolutionary combination, due to association. The development of Modern Industry, therefore, cuts from under its feet the very foundation on which the bourgeoisie produces and appropriates products. What the bourgeoisie, therefore, produces, above all, is its own grave-diggers. Its fall and the victory of the proletariat are equally inevitable.

In what relation do the Communists stand to the proletarians as a whole?

The Communists do not form a separate party opposed to other working-class parties.

They have no interests separate and apart from those of the proletariat as a whole.

They do not set up any sectarian principles of their own, by which to shape and mould the proletarian movement.

The Communists are distinguished from the other working-class parties by this only: 1. In the national struggles of the proletarians of the different countries, they point out and bring to the front the common interests of the entire proletariat, independently of all nationality. 2. In the various stages of development which the struggle of the working class against the bourgeoisie has to pass through, they always and everywhere represent the interests of the movement as a whole.

The Communists, therefore, are on the one hand, practically, the most advanced and resolute section of the working-class parties of every country, that section which pushes forward all others; on the other hand, theoretically, they have over the great mass of the proletariat the advantage of clearly understanding the line of march, the conditions, and the ultimate general results of the proletarian movement.

The immediate aim of the Communists is the same as that of all the other proletarian parties: formation of the proletariat into a class, overthrow of the bourgeois supremacy, conquest of political power by the proletariat.

. . . .The distinguishing feature of Communism is not the abolition of property generally, but the abolition of bourgeois property. But modern bourgeois private property is the final and most complete expression of the system of producing and appropriating products, that is based on class antagonisms, on the exploitation of the many by the few.

In this sense, the theory of the Communists may be summed up in the single sentence: Abolition of private property.

We Communists have been reproached with the desire of abolishing the right of personally acquiring property as the fruit of a man's own labour, which property is alledged to be the groundwork of all personal freedom, activity and independence.

Hard-won, self-acquired, self-earned property! Do you mean the property of the petty artisan and of the small peasant, a form of property that preceded the bourgeois form? There is no need to abolish that; the development of industry has to a great extent already destroyed it, and is still destroying it daily.

Or do you mean modern bourgeois private property?

But does wage-labour create any property for the labourer? Not a bit. It creates capital, i.e., that kind of property which exploits wage-labour, and which cannot increase except upon condition of begetting a new supply of wage-labour for fresh exploitation. Property, in its present form, is based on the antagonism of capital and wage-labour. Let us examine both sides of this antagonism.

To be a capitalist, is to have not only a purely personal, but a social *status* in production. Capital is a collective product, and only by the united action of many members, nay, in the last resort, only by the united action of all members of society, can it be set in motion.

Capital is, therefore, not a personal, it is a social power.

When, therefore, capital is converted into common property, into the property of all members of society, personal property is not thereby transformed into social property. It is only the social character of the property that is changed. It loses its class-character.

Let us now take wage-labour.

The average price of wage-labour is the minimum wage, i.e., the quantum of the means of subsistence, which is absolutely requisite to keep the labourer in bare existence as a labourer. What, therefore, the wage-labourer appropriates by means of his labour, merely suffices to prolong and reproduce a bare existence. We by no means intend to abolish this personal appropriation of the products of labour, an appropriation that is made for the maintenance and reproduction of human life, and that leaves no surplus wherewith to command the labour of others. All that we want to do away with, is the miserable character of this appropriation, under which the labourer lives merely to increase capital, and is allowed to live only in so far as the interest of the ruling class requires it.

In bourgeois society, living labour is but a means to increase accumulated labour. In Communist society, accumulated labour is but a means to widen, to enrich, to promote the existence of the labourer.

In bourgeois society, therefore, the past dominates the present; in Communist society, the present dominates the past. In bourgeois society capital is independent and has individuality, while the living person is dependent and has no individuality.

And the abolition of this state of things is called by the bourgeois, abolition of individuality and freedom! And rightly so. The abolition of bourgeois individuality, bourgeois independence, and bourgeois freedom is undoubtedly aimed at.

. . . .You are horrified at our intending to do away with private property. But in your existing society, private property is already done away with for nine-tenths of the population; its existence for the few is solely due to its non-existence in the hands of those nine-tenths. You reproach, us, therefore, with intending to do away with a form of property, the necessary condition for whose existence is, the non-existence of any property for the immense majority of society.

In one word, you reproach us with intending to do away with your property. Precisely so; that is just what we intend.

From the moment when labour can no longer be converted into capital, money, or rent, into a social power capable of being monopolised, i.e., from the moment when individual property can no longer be transformed into bourgeois property, into capital, from that moment, you say, individuality vanishes.

You must, therefore, confess that by "individual" you mean no other person than the middle-class owner of property. This person must, indeed, be swept out of the way, and made impossible.

Communism deprives no man of the power to appropriate the products of society; all that it does is to deprive him of the power to subjugate the labour of others by means of such appropriation.

. . . .The Communists are further reproached with desiring to abolish countries and nationality.

The working men have no country. We cannot take from them what they have not got. Since the proletariat must first of all acquire political supremacy, must rise to be the leading class of the nation, must constitute itself *the* nation, it is, so far, itself national, though not in the bourgeois sense of the word.

National differences and antagonisms between peoples are daily more and more vanishing, owing to the development of the bourgeoisie, to freedom of commerce, to the world-market, to uniformity in the mode of production and in the conditions of life corresponding thereto.

The supremacy of the proletariat will cause them to vanish still faster. United action, of the leading civilised countries at least, is one of the first conditions for the emancipation of the proletariat.

In proportion as the exploitation of one individual by another is put an end to, the exploitation of one nation by another will also be put an end to. In proportion as the antagonism between classes within the nation vanishes, the hostility of one nation to another will come to an end.

The charges against Communism made from a religious, a philosophical, and, generally, from an ideological standpoint, are not deserving of serious examination.

...The Communist revolution is the most radical rupture with traditional property relations; no wonder that its development involves the most radical rupture with traditional ideas.

But let us have done with the bourgeois objections to Communism.

...The first step in the revolution by the working class is to raise the proletariat to the position of ruling class, to win the battle of democracy.

The proletariat will use its political supremacy to wrest, by degrees, all capital from the bourgeoisie, to centralise all instruments of production in the hands of the State, i.e., of the proletariat organised as the ruling class; and to increase the total of productive forces as rapidly as possible.

Of course, in the beginning, this cannot be effected except by means of despotic inroads on the rights of property, and on the conditions of bourgeois production; by means of measures, therefore, which appear economically insufficient and untenable, but which, in the course of the movement, outstrip themselves, necessitate further inroads upon the old social order, and are unavoidable as a means of entirely revolutionising the mode of production.

These measures will of course be different in different countries.

Nevertheless in the most advanced countries, the following will be pretty generally applicable.

1. Abolition of property in land and application of all rents of land to public purposes.

2. A heavy progressive or graduated income tax.

3. Abolition of all right of inheritance.

4. Confiscation of the property of all emigrants and rebels.

5. Centralisation of credit in the hands of the State, by means of a national bank with State capital and an exclusive monopoly.

6. Centralisation of the means of communication and transport in the hands of the State.

7. Extension of factories and instruments of production owned by the State; the bringing into cultivation of waste-lands, and the improvement of the soil generally in accordance with a common plan.

8. Equal liability of all to labour. Establishment of industrial armies, especially for agriculture.

9. Combination of agriculture with manufacturing industries; gradual abolition of the distinction between town and country, by a more equable distribution of the population over the country.

10. Free education for all children in public schools. Abolition of children's factory labour in its present form. Combination of education with industrial production, etc., etc.

When, in the course of development, class distinctions have disappeared, and all production has been concentrated in the hands of a vast association of the whole nation, the public power will lose its political character. Political power, properly so called, is merely the organized power of one class for oppressing another. If the proletariat during its contest with the bourgeoisie is compelled, by the force of circumstances, to organize itself as a class, if, by means of a revolution, it makes itself ruling class, and, as such, sweeps away by force the old conditions of production, then it will, along with these conditions, have swept away the conditions for the existence of class antagonisms and of classes generally, and will thereby have abolished its own supremacy as a class.

In place of the old bourgeois society, with its classes and class antagonisms, we shall have an association, in which the free development of each is the condition for the free development of all.

...The Communists fight for the attainment of the immediate aims, for the enforcement of the momentary interests of the working class; but in the movement of the present, they also represent and take care of the future of that movement.

...the Communists everywhere support every revolutionary movement against the existing social and political order of things.

In all these movements they bring to the front, as the leading question in each, the property question, no matter what its degree of development at the time.

Finally, they labour everywhere for the union and agreement of the democratic parties of all countries.

The Communists disdain to conceal their views and aims. They openly declare that their ends can be attained only by the forcible overthrow of all existing social conditions. Let the ruling classes tremble at a Communistic revolution. The proletarians have nothing to lose but their chains. They have a world to win.

WORKING MEN OF ALL COUNTRIES, UNITE!

# leo tolstoy

Russian author, reformer, moral thinker and one of the world's greatest novelists, Leo Tolstoy was born on September 9, 1828, on the family estate at Yasnaya Polyana, about a hundred miles south of Moscow. Orphaned at nine, he was brought up by aunts and tutored in a fashion common to children of the Russian nobility. At the age of sixteen he entered the University of Kazan, but, disappointed with the instruction there, he returned to Yasnaya Polyana in 1847 to manage his estate and conduct his own education. His attempt at establishing a school for peasants on the family estate proved less than successful, and Tolstoy spent the next few years leading a wasteful life amidst the social circles of Moscow and St. Petersburg.

Disgusted with his shiftless existence, Tolstoy joined his soldier-brother Nikolai in the Caucasus in 1851; and in the following year, he joined the army himself and performed bravely in several engagements against the hill tribes. Much of his leisure time he spent in writing, completing his first published work, *Childhood,* in 1852. Transferred to the Danube front in 1854, Tolstoy participated in the siege of Sevastopol during the Crimean War. In notes kept during the next two years, he contrasted the simple heroism of the common soldier with the false heroics of his fellow officers. Some of these writings were published in a journal, *Contemporary,* and foreshadowed his later views on war. *War and Peace,* in which he gave even more eloquent form to these ideas, also grew out of his experiences at Sevastopol. At the end of the fighting in 1856, he left the army and went to St. Petersburg, where he became the idol of rival literary groups which sought his endorsement of their respective social and aesthetic views. Tolstoy by this date had become a pronounced individualist and, rather than pander to either party, he rebuffed both and left for the family estate at Yasnaya Polyana.

Tolstoy traveled abroad in 1857, visiting France, Switzerland, and Germany. His diary for this period reveals the remorseful soul-searching which he underwent as he began to question the bases of modern civilization. A renewed concern for the education of the poor prompted him once again to open a school for peasant children at the family estate. The success of his original teaching methods, which anticipated modern progressive education, drew him deeper into pedagogical studies. In 1860-61 he traveled to other parts of Western Europe, where he investigated educational theory and practice, and his subsequent texts and other publications in the field made him a renowned authority in the discipline.

Leo Tolstoy married Sophia Andreyevna Bers in 1862. Thereafter he dropped his educational activities and for the next fifteen years devoted himself to his marriage and to his family, which ultimately included thirteen children. During this period he wrote, among other things, *The Cossacks, War and Peace,* and *Anna Karenina,* all of which illustrate the author's view of history as a force proceeding inexorably toward its own end and depicts man as a helpless and accidental instrument.

A constant probing into the purpose of life, which had troubled him since his youth, eventually drove Tolstoy into a state of spiritual crisis. In or around 1876, he embraced the doctrine of Christian love and accepted the principle of nonresistance to evil. For the remainder of his life, Tolstoy preached his peculiar faith of non-violence and the simplistic, non-material life in books such as *What I Believe In* (1882). His new convictions took a form of Christian anarchism which led him to disavow immortality and reject the authority of the church. By 1901, the Russian Orthodox Church had become sufficiently provoked by his writings and teachings that it excommunicated him.

Following his "conversion," Tolstoy strove to live the life he preached. He gave up smoking and drinking, became a vegetarian, and frequently dressed in common peasant clothes. Since he also condemned private property, he would have preferred to donate his entire estate to the needs of the poor, but his family took legal action to prevent such a move. Believing that no one should exist on the labors of others, Tolstoy became as self-sufficient as possible, cleaning his own room, working in the fields, and making some of his own clothes. His asceticism extended to his sexual relations with his wife, who by this time was almost totally estranged from him anyway. She, and all of the children except the youngest daughter Alexandra, resented the strange types of people who became Tolstoy's adherents and who frequently sought him out at his home. Many of his followers set up communes in order to live together according to their "Leader's" precepts. But Tolstoy distrusted such organized efforts and kept insisting that the truth that brings happiness can only be achieved by individuals who honestly look within themselves.

All of the excerpts which follow were written in this latter part of Tolstoy's life, and they keenly reflect his moral and social concepts. The first selection reveals Tolstoy's reaction to the establishment of the Nobel Peace Prize and his judgement that the Dukhobors would make deserving recipients of such an award. The Dukhobors were a pacifist sect persecuted by the Russian government. Indeed, while nearly all monies earned from his many publications went to the family following Tolstoy's voluntary transfer of his legacy to them, he did retain the income from his last long novel, *Resurrection* (1899), and he promptly donated it to the Dukhobors.

A second selection, "Letter to a Corporal" (1899), is a scathing attack against all forms of military service, which his own experience had taught him to hate so intensely. Whatever the merits of his arguments, they certainly embody as much relevance today as they did at the time in which they were written.

The final selection, "Patriotism and Government," was published only six months before his death and contains a preface by Ernest Belfort Bax. Ernest Bax (1854-1926) was a co-founder, with William Morris, of the Socialist League in Britain in 1885; Bax's own socialist beliefs tended toward anarchism. Tolstoy's theme in this particular essay is the folly of patriotism, particularly the more perverse forms of jingoistic and chauvinistic patriotism. His remarks, written in 1910, seem no less suitable for the world of the 1970s.

The aging Tolstoy was profoundly troubled in the last days of his life by the embarrassing and painful contradiction between the simplistic life he preached, and the life of ease and creature comforts which surrounded him at the family estate. Finally, with domestic relations progressively deteriorating, he left home stealthily one night, accompanied by his youngest daughter, Alexandra, in search of a place where he could rest quietly and come closer to God. A few days later, on November 20, 1910, he died of pneumonia at the remote railway junction of Astapovo, in the province of Ryazan. The forlorn home in which he was to die was less than a hundred miles from the home in which he could not live.

## Nobel's Bequest

I read in some Swedish papers that by Nobel's will a certain sum of money is bequeathed to him who shall most serve the cause of peace.

I assume that the men who served the cause of peace did so only because they served God; and every monetary reward can only be disagreeable to them, in that it gives a selfish character to their service of God. For this reason it would seem that this condition of Nobel's will can hardly be executed correctly. Indeed, it cannot be correctly executed in relation to the men themselves who have all the time served the cause of peace; but, I presume, it will be quite correctly executed, if the money shall be distributed among the families of those men who have served the cause of peace and in consequence of this service are in a most difficult and wretched condition. I am speaking of the families of the Dukhobors of the Caucasus, who, to the number of four thousand people, have been suffering these three years from the Russian government's severe treatment of them, because their husbands, sons, and fathers refuse to do active or reserve military service.

Thirty-two of those who have refused have, after having stayed in the disciplinary battalion, where two of them died, been sent to the worst parts of Siberia, and about three hundred men are pining away in the prisons of the Caucasus and of Russia.

The incompatibility of military service with the profession of Christianity has always been clear for all true Christians, and has many times been expressed by them; but the church sophists, who are in the service of the authorities, have always known how to drown these voices, so that simple people have not seen this incompatibility and, continuing to call themselves Christians, have entered military service and have obeyed the authorities, which practised them in acts of murder, but the contradiction between the profession of Christianity and the participation in military matters has become more obvious with every day, and finally, in our day, when, on the one hand, the amicable communion and unity of the Christian nations is growing more and more intimate and, on the other, these same nations are more and more burdened with terrible armaments for mutually hostile purposes, it has reached the utmost degree of tension. Everybody speaks of peace, and peace is preached by the preachers and pastors in their churches, by the peace societies in their gatherings, by writers in newspapers and books, by representatives of the government—in their speeches, toasts, and all kinds of demonstrations. Everybody speaks and writes about peace, but nobody believes in it and nobody can believe in it, because these same

From Count Leo N. Tolstoy, "Miscellaneous Letters and Essays," translated and edited by Leo Wiener, in *The Complete Works of Count Tolstoy*, XXIII, Colonial Press Company, New York, 1905, pp. 332-337. This essay is dated August 29, 1897.

preachers and pastors, who to-day preach against war, to-morrow bless the flags and cannon and, extolling the commanders, welcome their armies; the members of the peace societies, their orators and writers against war, as soon as their turns come, calmly enter the military caste and prepare themselves for murder; the emperors and kings, who yesterday solemnly assured all men that they are concerned only about peace, the next day exercise their troops for murder and boast to one another of their well-prepared multitudes armed for murder, and so the voices, raised amidst this universal lie, by men who actually want peace, and show not only in words, but also in their acts, that they really want it, cannot help but be heard. These people say: "We are Christians, and so we cannot agree to being murderers. You may kill and torture us, but we will still refuse to be murderers, because that is contrary to that same Christianity which you profess."

. . . These words again point out to the world that simple, indubitable, and only means for the establishment of actual peace which was long ago pointed out by Christ, but which has been so forgotten by men that they on all sides search for means for the establishment of peace, and have no recourse to the one, long familiar method, which is so simple that for its application nothing new has to be undertaken, but we need only stop doing what we always and for everybody consider to be bad and disgraceful,—if we stop being submissive slaves of those who prepare men for murder. Not only is this method simple,—it is also indubitable. Any other method for the establishment of peace may be doubtful, but not this one, with which men who profess Christianity recognize, what no one has ever doubted, that a Christian cannot be a murderer. And Christians need only recognize what they cannot help recognizing, and there will be eternal inviolable peace among all Christians. Not only is the method simple and indubitable,—it is also the only method for the establishment of peace among Christians. It is the only one, because, so long as Christians will recognize the possibility of their taking part in military service, so long will the armies be in the power of the governments; and so long as they shall be in the power of the governments, there will be wars.

. . . The Dukhobors look upon their ruin, their want, imprisonment, and deportations as the work of serving God, and do this service with pride and joy, concealing nothing and fearing nothing, because nothing worse can be done to them unless they be put to death, which they do not fear.

But not such is the condition of the Russian government. If we, who are deceived by the government, do not see the whole significance of what the Dukhobors are doing, the government does see it; it not only sees the danger, but also the hopelessness of its position. It sees that as soon as people shall be freed from that spell under which they are now, and shall understand that a Christian cannot be a soldier,—and this they cannot help but understand,—and as soon as they hear what the Dukhobors did, the government will have inevitably to renounce, either Christianity,—and the governments rule in the name of Christianity—or its power. The government is in relation to the Dukhobors in a desperate state. They cannot be left alone, for all the rest will do likewise; nor is it possible to destroy them, to lock them up forever, as is done with individuals who interfere with the government—there are too many of them; the old men, wives, children, not only do not dissuade their fathers and husbands, but encourage them in their determination. What is to be done?

And so the government tries secretly, murderously, to destroy these men and to make them harmless, by keeping the men in solitary confinement, with the greatest secrecy, forbidding outsiders to commune with them, and by sending them to the most remote regions of Siberia, among the Yakuts; their families it deports among the Tartars and Georgians: it does not admit any one to them and forbids the printing of any information about the Dukhobors, and commands its accomplices to print all kinds of calumnies against them. But all these methods are inefficient. The light shineth in the dark. It is impossible at once to wipe off from the face of the earth a population of four thousand people who command the respect of all men; if they shall die out under the conditions in which they are placed, this extinction is slow, and extinction for the profession of the truth amidst other people is a most powerful sermon, and this sermon is being carried farther and farther. The government knows this and yet cannot help doing what it is doing; but we can already see on whose side is the victory.

It is this pointing out of the weakness of violence and of the power of truth which is in our time the great . . . [contribution] of the Dukhobors in the matter of the establishment of peace. For this reason I think that no one has more than they served the cause of peace, and the unfortunate conditions under which their families are living . . . are the reason why the money which Nobel wished should be given to those who more than any one else served the cause of peace could not be adjudged to any one with greater justice than to these very Dukhobor families.

## Letter to a Corporal

You wonder how it is soldiers are taught that it is right to kill men in certain cases and in war, whereas in the Scripture, which is acknowledged to be sacred

From *The Complete Works of Count Tolstoy*, XXIII, pp. 449-456. The letter was written in 1889.

by those who teach this, there is nothing resembling such a permission, but there is the very opposite,—a prohibition to commit murder and even any insult against men, a prohibition to do to others what one does not wish to have done to oneself; you ask me whether this is not a deception, and if so, for whose advantage it is practised.

Yes, it is a deception, which is practised in favour of those who are accustomed to live by the sweat and blood of other people, and who for this purpose have been distorting Christ's teaching, which was given men for their good, but which now, in its distorted form, has become the chief source of all the calamities of men.

This happened in the following way:

The government and all those men of the upper classes who adhere to the government and live by the labours of others have to have means for controlling the labouring masses; the army is such a means. The defence against foreign enemies is only an excuse. The German government frightens its nation with the Russians and the French; the French frightens its nation with the Germans; the Russian frightens its nation with the Germans and the French, and so it is with all the nations; but neither the Germans, nor the Russians, nor the French wish to fight with their neighbours and with other nations; they prefer to live in peace with them and are afraid of war more than of anything in the world. But, to have an excuse in their control of the labouring masses, the governments and the upper idle classes act like a gypsy, who ships his horse around the corner and then pretends that he is not able to hold it back. They stir up their people and another government, and then pretend that for the good or for the defence of their nation they cannot help but declare war, which again is profitable for the generals, officers, officials, merchants, and, in general, for the wealthy classes. In reality, war is only an inevitable consequence of the existence of the armies; but the armies are needed by the governments merely for the purpose of controlling their own labouring masses.

...The masses are crushed, robbed, impoverished, ignorant,—they are dying out. Why? Because the land is in the hands of the rich; because the masses are enslaved in factories, in plants, in their daily occupations; because they are fleeced for the taxes, and the price for their labour is lowered, and the price for what they need is raised. How can they be freed? Shall the land again be taken away from the rich? But if that is done, the soldiers will come, will kill off the rioters, and will lock them up in prisons. Shall the factories, the plants, be taken away? The same will happen. Stick out in a strike? But that will never happen,—the rich can stick out longer than the labourers, and the armies will always be on the side of the capitalists. The masses will never get away from that want in which they are held, so long as the armies shall be in the power of the ruling classes.

But who are the armies, which hold the masses in this slavery? Who are those soldiers who will shoot at the peasants who have taken possession of the land, and at the strikers, if they do not disperse, and at the smugglers, who import wares without paying the revenue,—who will put into prisons and keep there those who refuse to pay the taxes? These soldiers are the same peasants whose land has been taken away, the same strikers, who want to raise their wages, the same payers of the taxes, who want to be freed from these payments.

Why do these men shoot at their brothers? Because it has been impressed upon them that the oath which they are compelled to take upon entering military service is obligatory for them, and that they may not kill men in general, but may kill them by command of the authorities, that is, the same deception which startled so much is practised upon them. But here arises the question,—how can people of sound mind, who frequently know the rudiments and are even educated, believe in such a palpable lie? No matter how little educated a man may be, he none the less cannot help knowing that Christ did not permit any murder, but taught meekness, humility, forgiveness of offences, love of enemies; he cannot help but see that on the basis of the Christian teaching he cannot make a promise in advance that he will kill all those whom he is commanded to kill.

The question is, how can people of sound mind believe, as all those who are now doing military service have believed, in such an obvious deception? The answer to the question is this, that people are not deceived by this one deception alone, but have been prepared for it from childhood by a whole series of deceptions, a whole system of deceptions, which is called the Orthodox Church, and which is nothing but the coarsest kind of idolatry.

...Only a man who is completely stupified by that false faith, called Orthodox, which is given out to him as being Christian, is able to believe that it is no sin for a Christian to enter the army, promising blindly to obey any man who will consider himself higher in rank, and, at the command of another man, to learn to kill and to commit this most terrible crime, which is prohibited by all the laws.

... By making use of the power which it has, the government produces and maintains the deception, and the deception maintains its power.

And so the only means for freeing men from all the calamities consists in freeing them from that false faith which is inculcated upon them by the government, and in impressing upon them the true Christian teaching, which is concealed from them by this false doctrine.

... It is impossible to fill a vessel with what is important if it is already filled with what is useless. It is necessary first to pour out what is useless. Even so it is with the acquisition of the true Christian teaching. We must first understand that all the stories about how God created the world six thousand years ago, and how

Adam sinned, and how the human race fell, and how the son of God and God Himself, born of a virgin, came into the world and redeemed it, and all the fables of the Bible and of the Gospel, and all the lives of the saints, and the stories of miracles and relics, are nothing but a coarse mixing up of the superstitions of the Jewish nation with the deceptions of the clergy. Only for a man who is completely free from these deceptions can the simple and clear teaching of Christ, which demands no interpretations and is self-comprehensible, be accessible and comprehensible.

This teaching says nothing about the beginning or the end of the world, nor of God and His intentions, in general nothing about what we cannot know and need not know, but speaks only of what a man has to do in order to be saved, that is, in order in the best manner possible to pass the life into which he has come in this world, from his birth to his death. For this purpose we need only treat others as we wish to be treated. In this alone does the law and the prophets consist, as Christ has said. To do so, we need no images, no relics, no divine services, no priests, no sacred histories, no catechisms, no governments, but, on the contrary, a liberation from all that—because only the man who is free from those fables which the priests give out to him as the only truth, and who is not bound to other people by promises to act as they want him to act, can treat others as he wishes to be treated by them. Only in that case will a man be able to do, not his own will, nor that of others, but the will of God.

But the will of God consists, not in fighting and oppressing others, but in recognizing all men as brothers and serving one another.

## Patriotism and Government

*The time is fast approaching when to call a man a patriot will be the deepest insult you can offer him. Patriotism now means advocating plunder in the interests of the privileged classes of the particular State system into which we have happened to be born.*

I have already several times expressed the thought that in our day the feeling of patriotism is an unnatural, irrational, and harmful feeling, and a cause of a great part of the ills from which mankind is suffering; and that, consequently, this

From Leo Tolstoy, *Essays and Letters*, translated by Aylmer Maude, Funk and Wagnalls Company, New York, 1904, pp. 238-240, 243-245, 251-253, 257-261. This essay is dated May 10, 1910.

feeling should not be cultivated, as is now being done, but should, on the contrary, be suppressed and eradicated by all means available to rational men. Yet, strange to say—though it is undeniable that the universal armaments and destructive wars which are ruining the peoples result from that one feeling—all my arguments showing the backwardness, anachronism, and harmfulness of patriotism have been met, and are still met, either by silence, by intentional misinterpretation, or by a strange unvarying reply to the effect that only bad patriotism (Jingoism, or Chauvinism) is evil, but that real good patriotism is a very elevated moral feeling, to condemn which is not only irrational but wicked.

What this real, good patriotism consists in, we are never told; or, if anything is said about it, instead of explanation we get declamatory, inflated phrases, or, finally, some other conception is substituted for patriotism—something which has nothing in common with the patriotism we all know, and from the results of which we all suffer so severely.

... the real patriotism, which we all know, by which most people to-day are swayed, and from which humanity suffers so severely, is not the wish for spiritual benefits for one's own people (it is impossible to desire spiritual benefits for one's own people only), but is a very definite feeling of preference for one's own people or State above all other peoples and States, and a consequent wish to get for that people or State the greatest advantages and power that can be got—things which are obtainable only at the expense of the advantages and power of other peoples or States.

It would, therefore, seem obvious that patriotism as a feeling is bad and harmful, and as a doctrine is stupid. For it is clear that if each people and each State considers itself the best of peoples and States, they all live in a gross and harmful delusion.

... Patriotism, as a feeling of exclusive love for one's own people, and as a doctrine of the virtue of sacrificing one's tranquillity, one's property, and even one's life, in defence of one's own people from slaughter and outrage by their enemies, was the highest idea of the period when each nation considered it feasible and just, for its own advantage, to subject to slaughter and outrage the people of other nations.

But, already some 2,000 years ago, humanity, in the person of the highest representatives of its wisdom, began to recognize the higher idea of a brotherhood of man; and that idea, penetrating man's consciousness more and more, has in our time attained most varied forms of realization. Thanks to improved means of communication, and to the unity of industry, of trade, of the arts, and of science, men are to-day so bound one to another that the danger of conquest, massacre, or outrage by a neighbouring people, has quite disappeared, and all peoples (the peoples, but not the Governments) live together in peaceful, mutually advantageous, and friendly commercial, industrial, artistic, and scientific relations, which they have no need and no desire to disturb. One would think, therefore, that the antiquated feeling of patriotism—being superfluous and incompatible with the consciousness we have reached of the existence of brotherhood among men of different nationalities—should dwindle more and more until it completely disappears. Yet the very opposite of this occurs: this harmful and antiquated feeling not only continues to exist, but burns more and more fiercely.

The peoples, without any reasonable ground, and contrary alike to their conception of right and to their own advantage, not only sympathize with Governments in their attacks on other nations, in their seizures of foreign possessions, and in defending by force what they have already stolen, but even themselves demand such attacks, seizures, and defences: are glad of them, and take pride in them. The small oppressed nationalities which have fallen under the power of the great States—the Poles, Irish, Bohemians, Finns, or Armenians—resenting the patriotism of their conquerors, which is the cause of their oppression, catch from them the infection of this feeling of patriotism—which has ceased to be necessary, and is now obsolete, unmeaning, and harmful—and catch it to such a degree that all their activity is concentrated upon it, and they, themselves suffering from the patriotism of the stronger nations, are ready, for the sake of patriotism, to perpetrate on other peoples the very same deeds that their oppressors have perpetrated and are perpetrating on them.

This occurs because the ruling classes (including not only the actual rulers with their officials, but all the classes who enjoy an exceptionally advantageous position: the capitalists, journalists, and most of the artists and scientists) can retain their position—exceptionally advantageous in comparison with that of the labouring masses—thanks only to the Government organization, which rests on patriotism. They have in their hands all the most powerful means of influencing the people, and always sedulously support patriotic feelings in themselves and in others, more especially as those feelings which uphold the Government's power are those that are always best rewarded by that power.

Every official prospers the more in his career, the more patriotic he is; so also the army man gets promotion in time of war—the war is produced by patriotism.

Patriotism and its result—wars—give an enormous revenue to the newspaper trade, and profits to many other trades. Every writer, teacher, and professor is more secure in his place the more he preaches patriotism. Every Emperor and King obtains the more fame the more he is addicted to patriotism.

The ruling classes have in their hand the army, money, the schools, the churches, and the press. In the schools they kindle patriotism in the children by means of histories describing their own people as the best of all peoples and always in the right. Among adults they kindle it by spectacles, jubilees, monuments, and by a lying patriotic press. Above all, they inflame patriotism in this way: perpetrating every kind of injustice and harshness against other nations, they provoke in them enmity towards their own people, and then in turn exploit that enmity to embitter their people against the foreigner.

The intensification of this terrible feeling of patriotism has gone on among the European peoples in a rapidly increasing progression, and in our time has reached the utmost limits, beyond which there is no room for it to extend.

. . . The Government, in the widest sense, including capitalists and the Press, is nothing else than an organization which places the greater part of the people in the power of a smaller part, who dominate them; that smaller part is subject to a yet smaller part, and that again to a yet smaller, and so on, reaching at last a few people, or one single man, who by means of military force has.power over all the rest. So that all this organization resembles a cone, of which all the parts are completely in the power of those people, or of that one person, who happens to be at the apex.

The apex of the cone is seized by those who are more cunning, audacious, and unscrupulous than the rest, or by someone who happens to be the heir of those who were audacious and unscrupulous.

. . . And to such Governments is allowed full power, not only over property and lives, but even over the spiritual and moral development, the education, and the religious guidance of everybody.

People construct such a terrible machine of power, they allow anyone to seize it who can (and the chances always are that it will be seized by the most morally worthless)—they slavishly submit to him, and are then surprised, that evil comes of it. They are afraid of Anarchists' bombs, and are not afraid of this terrible organization which is always threatening them with the greatest calamities.

. . . To deliver men from the terrible and ever-increasing evils of armaments and wars, we want neither congresses nor conferences, nor treaties, nor courts of arbitration, but the destruction of those instruments of violence which are called Governments, and from which humanity's greatest evils flow.

To destroy Governmental *violence*, only one thing is needed: it is that people should understand that the feeling of patriotism, which alone supports that instrument of violence, is a rude, harmful, disgraceful, and bad feeling, and, above all, is immoral. It is a rude feeling, because it is one natural only to people standing on the lowest level of morality, and expecting from other nations such outrages as they themselves are ready to inflict; it is a harmful feeling, because it disturbs advantageous and joyous, peaceful relations with other peoples, and above all produces that Governmental organization under which power may fall, and does fall, into the hands of the worst men; it is a disgraceful feeling, because it turns man not merely into a slave, but into a fighting cock, a bull, or a gladiator, who wastes his strength and his life for objects which are not his own but his Governments'; and it is an immoral feeling, because, instead of confessing one's self a son of God (as Christianity teaches us) or even a free man guided by his own reason, each man under the influence of patriotism confesses himself the son of his fatherland and the slave of his Government, and commits actions contrary to his reason and his conscience.

It is only necessary that people should understand this, and the terrible bond, called Government, by which we are chained together, will fall to pieces of itself without struggle; and with it will cease the terrible and useless evils it produces.

. . . 'But' it is usually asked, 'what will there be instead of Governments?'

There will be nothing. Something that has long been useless and therefore superfluous and bad, will be abolished. An organ that, being unnecessary, has become harmful, will be abolished.

'But,' people generally say, 'if there is no Government, people will violate and kill each other.'

Why? Why should the abolition of the organization which arose in consequence of violence, and which has been handed down from generation to generation to do violence—why should the abolition of such an organization, now devoid of use, cause people to outrage and kill one another? On the contrary, the presumption is that the abolition of the organ of violence would result in people ceasing to violate and kill one another.

Now, some men are specially educated and trained to kill and to do violence to other people—there are men who are supposed to have a right to use violence, and who make use of an organization which exists for that purpose. Such deeds of violence and such killing are considered good and worthy deeds.

But then, people will not be so brought up, and no one will have a right to use violence to others, and there will be no organization to do violence, and—as is natural to people of our time—violence and murder will always be considered bad actions, no matter who commits them.

But should acts of violence continue to be committed even after the abolition of the Governments, such acts will certainly be fewer than are committed now, when an organization exists specially devised to commit acts of violence, and a state of things exists in which acts of violence and murders are considered good and useful deeds.

The abolition of Governments will merely rid us of an unnecessary organization which we have inherited from the past, an organization for the commission of violence and for its justification.

'But there will then be no laws, no property, no courts of justice, no police, no popular education,' say people who intentionally confuse the use of violence by Governments with various social activities.

The abolition of the organization of Government formed to do violence, does not at all involve the abolition of what is reasonable and good, and therefore not based on violence, in laws or law courts, or in property, or in police regulations, or in financial arrangements, or in popular education. On the contrary, the absence of the brutal power of Government, which is needed only for its own support, will facilitate a juster and more reasonable social organization, needing no violence. Courts of justice, and public affairs, and popular education, will all exist to the extent to which they are really needed by the people, but in a shape which will not involve the evils contained in the present form of Government. Only that will be destroyed which was evil and hindered the free expression of the people's will.

But even if we assume that with the absence of Governments there would be disturbances and civil strife, even then the position of the people would be better than it is at present. The position now is such that it is difficult to imagine anything worse. The people are ruined, and their ruin is becoming more and more complete. The men are all converted into warslaves, and have from day to day to expect orders to go to kill and to be killed. What more? Are the ruined peoples to die of hunger? Even that is already beginning in Russia, in Italy, and in India. Or are the women as well as the men to go to be soldiers? In the Transvaal even that has begun.

So that even if the absence of Government really meant Anarchy in the negative, disorderly sense of that word—which is far from being the case—even then no anarchical disorder could be worse than the position to which Governments have already led their peoples, and to which they are leading them.

And therefore emancipation from patriotism, and the destruction of the despotism of Government that rests upon it, cannot but be beneficial to mankind.

Men, recollect yourselves! For the sake of your well-being, physical and spiritual, for the sake of your brothers and sisters, pause, consider, and think of what you are doing!

Reflect, and you will understand that your foes are not the Boers, or the English, or the French, or the Germans, or the Finns, or the Russians, but that your foes—your only foes—are you yourselves, who by your patriotism maintain the Governments that oppress you and make you unhappy.

They have undertaken to protect you from danger, and they have brought that pseudo-protection to such a point that you have all become soldiers—slaves, and are all ruined, or are being ruined more and more, and at any moment may and should expect that the tight-stretched cord will snap, and a horrible slaughter of you and your children will commence.

And however great that slaughter may be, and however that conflict may end, the same state of things will continue. In the same way, and with yet greater intensity, the Governments will arm, and ruin, and pervert you and your children, and no one will help you to stop it or to prevent it, if you do not help yourselves.

And there is only one kind of help possible—it lies in the abolition of that terrible linking up into a cone of violence, which enables the person or persons who succeed in seizing the apex to have power over all the rest, and to hold that power the more firmly the more cruel and inhuman they are, as we see by the cases of the Napoleons, Nicholas I., Bismarck, Chamberlain, Rhodes, and our Russian Dictators who rule the people in the Tsar's name.

And there is only one way to destroy this binding together—it is by shaking off the hypnotism of patriotism.

Understand that all the evils from which you suffer, you yourselves cause by yielding to the suggestions by which Emperors, Kings, Members of Parliament, Governors, officers, capitalists, priests, authors, artists, and all who need this fraud of patriotism in order to live upon your labour, deceive you!

Whoever you may be—Frenchman, Russian, Pole, Englishman, Irishman, or Bohemian—understand that all your real human interests, whatever they may be—agricultural, industrial, commercial, artistic, or scientific—as well as your pleasures and joys, in no way run counter to the interests of other peoples or States; and that you are united, by mutual co-operation, by interchange of services, by the joy of wide brotherly intercourse, and by the interchange not merely of goods but also of thoughts and feelings, with the folk of other lands.

Understand that the question as to who manages to seize Wei-hai-wei, Port Arthur, or Cuba—your Government or another—does not affect you, or, rather, that every seizure made by your Government injures you, by inevitably bringing in its train all sorts of pressure on you by your government to force you to take part in the robbery and violence by which alone such seizures are made, or can be retained when made. Understand that your life can in no way be bettered by Alsace becoming German or French, and Ireland or Poland being free or enslaved—whoever holds them. You are free to live where you will, if even you be an Alsatian, an Irishman, or a Pole. Understand, too, that by stirring up patriotism you will only make the case worse, for the subjection in which your people are kept has resulted simply from the struggle between patriotisms, and every manifestation of patriotism in one nation provokes a corresponding reaction in another. Understand that salvation from your woes is only possible when you free yourself from the obsolete idea of patriotism and from the obedience to Governments that is based upon it, and when you boldly enter into the region of that higher idea, the brotherly union of the peoples, which has long since come to life, and from all sides is calling you to itself.

If people would but understand that they are not the sons of some fatherland or other, nor of Governments, but are sons of God, and can therefore neither be slaves nor enemies one to another—those insane, unnecessary, worn-out, pernicious organizations called Governments, and all the sufferings, violations, humiliations, and crimes which they occasion, would cease.

NOTES

# william morris

An English poet, artist, and printer, William Morris's interest in social reform was largely inspired by his hatred of the ugliness and soul-destroying effects which derived from the industrial revolution in nineteenth century Britain. Morris likened the capitalist system to a modern day form of slavery, equated the principle of competition with war, and proposed revolutionary social changes which he hoped could be accomplished without violence and destruction. Such an outcome would be possible, he thought, if the propertied classes recognized the futility of defending a thoroughly corrupt system, already in a state of decay, and consented gracefully to the changes required in providing equity and justice for everyone.

The eldest son of affluent parents, William Morris was born March 24, 1834, at Walthamstow, Essex, and was educated at Exeter College, Oxford. After graduation in 1855, Morris pursued his primary interest, architecture; he was also encouraged to paint and to write by Dante Gabriel Rossetti, the English poet and artist whose paintings of Morris's wife, Jane Burden, won wide acclaim. Morris's work as a decorator and designer revolutionized Victorian tastes; his reading of English critic and social theorist John Ruskin revolutionized his thought. Although neither politics nor writing interfered with his professional productivity as an artist, Morris devoted considerable energies to the Socialist cause.

Disillusioned with the Liberal Party's position on the Irish question and on a number of other serious domestic problems, Morris joined the Social Democratic federation in 1883. He became a leader of the Socialist League, formed the following year, as well as editor of its journal *The Commonweal.* Morris advocated socialist doctrines in his writings and lectures, and at meetings in industrial towns. He was arrested in 1885, and again in 1887 following a meeting in Trafalgar Square which was violently dispersed by London police on "Bloody Sunday" (November 13).

It was the Socialist League's increasing anarchist sympathies which prompted Morris to withdraw from the organization in 1890, but he remained committed to the Socialist cause and wrote and lectured widely on the relation of art to industry. His goal was a Socialist commonwealth where simplicity and happiness reigned. In his book *News from Nowhere,* Morris depicted his ideal society based upon the concept of joy in labor, with "useful work" replacing "useless toil." He believed in equality based upon a sense of mutual responsiblity between master and worker. The following selection is taken from a volume of his collected works and, like much of his writing, it reflects timeless moral lessons unmarred by active political propaganda.

William Morris spent his last years in Hammersmith, where he died on October 3, 1896. He was survived by his widow, Jane, and his two daughters, Jenny and May. The latter devoted herself to her father's memory and published his collected works in twenty-four volumes (1910-1915).

## On the Coming of Socialism

The word Revolution, which we Socialists are so often forced to use, has a terrible sound in most people's ears, even when we have explained to them that it does not necessarily mean a change accompanied by riot and all kinds of violence, and cannot mean a change made mechanically and in the teeth of opinion by a group of men who have somehow managed to seize on the executive power for the moment. Even when we explain that we use the word revolution in its etymological sense, and mean by it a change in the basis of society, people are scared at the idea of such a vast change, and beg that you will speak of reform and not revolution. As, however, we Socialists do not at all mean by

From *The Collected Works of William Morris,* XXIII, Longmans Green and Company, London, 1915, pp. 3, 5, 7, 13-14, 20, 22-23, 26, 73-80.

our word revolution what these worthy people mean by their word reform, I can't help thinking that it would be a mistake to use it, whatever projects we might conceal beneath its harmless envelope. So we will stick to our word, which means a change of the basis of society; it may frighten people, but it will at least warn them that there is something to be frightened about, which will be no less dangerous for being ignored; and also it may encourage some people, and will mean to them at least not a fear, but a hope.

Fear and Hope—those are the names of the two great passions which rule the race of man, and with which revolutionists have to deal; to give hope to the many oppressed and fear to the few oppressors, that is our business; if we do the first and give hope to the many, the few *must* be frightened by their hope; otherwise we do not want to frighten them; it is not revenge we want for poor people, but happiness; indeed, what revenge can be taken for all the thousands of years of the sufferings of the poor?

. . . How do we live, then, under our present system? Let us look at it a little.

And first, please to understand that our present system of Society is based on a state of perpetual war. Do any of you think that this is as it should be? I know that you have often been told that the competition which is at present the rule of all production, is a good thing, and stimulates the progress of the race; but the people who tell you this should call competition by its shorter name of *war* if they wish to be honest, and you would then be free to consider whether or not war stimulates progress, otherwise than as a mad bull chasing you over your own garden may do. War, or competition, whichever you please to call it, means at the best pursuing your own advantage at the cost of some one else's loss, and in the process of it you must not be sparing of destruction even of your own possessions, or you will certainly come by the worse in the struggle. You understand that perfectly as to the kind of war in which people go out to kill and be killed; that sort of war in which ships are commissioned, for instance, "to sink, burn, and destroy;" but it appears that you are not so conscious of this waste of goods when you are only carrying on that other war called *commerce*; observe, however, that the waste is there all the same.

. . . Well, surely Socialism can offer you something in the place of all that. It can; it can offer you peace and friendship instead of war. We might live utterly without national rivalries, acknowledging that while it is best for those who feel that they naturally form a community under one name to govern themselves, yet that no community in civilization should feel that it had interests opposed to any other, their economical condition being at any rate similar; so that any citizen of one community could fall to work and live without disturbance of his life when he was in a foreign country, and would fit into his place quite naturally; so that all civilized nations would form one great community, agreeing together as to the kind and amount of production and distribution needed; working at such and such production where it could be best produced; avoiding waste by all means. Please to think of the amount of waste which they would avoid, how much such a revolution would add to the wealth of the world! What creature on earth would be harmed by such a revolution? Nay, would not everybody be the better for it?

...what Socialism offers you in place of ... artificial famines, with their so-called over-production is, once more, regulation of the markets, supply and demand commensurate; no gambling, and consequently (once more) no waste; not overwork and weariness for the worker one month, and the next no work and terror of starvation, but steady work and plenty of leisure every month; not cheap market wares, that is to say, adulterated wares with scarcely any *good* in them, mere scaffold-poles for building up profits; no labour would be spent on such things as these, which people would cease to want when they ceased to be slaves. Not these, but such goods as best fulfilled the real uses of the consumers would labour be set to make; for profit being abolished, people could have what they wanted, instead of what the profit-grinders at home and abroad forced them to take.

For what I want you to understand is this: that in every civilized country at least there is plenty for all—is, or at any rate might be. Even with labour so misdirected as it is at present, an equitable distribution of the wealth we have would make all people comparatively comfortable; but that is nothing to the wealth we might have if labour were not misdirected.

... even that share of work necessary to the existence of the simplest social life must, in the first place, whatever else it is, be reasonable work; that is, it must be such work as a good citizen can see the necessity for; as a member of the community, I must have agreed to do it.

To take two strong instances of the contrary, I won't submit to be dressed up in red and marched off to shoot at my French or German or Arab friend in a quarrel that I don't understand; I will rebel sooner than do that.

Nor will I submit to waste my time and energies in making some trifling toy which I know only a fool can desire: I will rebel sooner than do that.

However, you may be sure that in a state of social order I shall have no need to rebel against any such pieces of unreason; only I am forced to speak from the way we live to the way we might live.

... And once for all, there is nothing in our circumstances save the hunting of profit that drives us into it. It is profit which draws men into enormous unmanageable aggregations called towns, for instance; profit which crowds them up when they are there into quarters without gardens or open spaces; profit which won't take the most ordinary precautions against wrapping a whole district in a cloud of sulphurous smoke; which turns beautiful rivers into filthy sewers; which condemns all but the rich to live in houses idiotically cramped and confined at the best, and at the worst in houses for whose wretchedness there is no name.

I say it is almost incredible that we should bear such crass stupidity as this; nor should we if we could help it. We shall not bear it when the workers get out of their heads that they are but an appendage to profit-grinding, that the more profits that are made the more employment at high wages there will be for them, and that therefore all the incredible filth, disorder, and degradation of modern civilization are signs of their prosperity. So far from that, they are signs of their slavery. When they are no longer slaves they will claim as a matter of course that every man and every family should be generously lodged; that every child should be able to play in a garden close to the place his parents live in; that the houses should by their obvious decency and order be ornaments to Nature, not disfigurements of it; for the decency and order above-mentioned when carried to the due pitch would most assuredly lead to beauty in building. All this, of course, would mean the people—that is, all society—duly organized, having in its own hands the means of production, to be *owned* by no individual, but used by all as occasion called for its use, and can only be done on those terms; on any other terms people will be driven to accumulate private wealth for themselves, and thus, as we have seen, to waste the goods of the community and perpetuate the division into classes, which means continual war and waste.

. . . Hard as the work is, however, its reward is not doubtful. The mere fact that a body of men, however small, are banded together as Socialist missionaries shows that the change is going on. As the working-classes, the real organic part of society, take in these ideas, hope will arise in them, and they will claim changes in society, many of which doubtless will not tend directly towards their emancipation, because they will be claimed without due knowledge of the one thing necessary to claim, *equality of condition;* but which indirectly will help to break up our rotten sham society, while that claim for equality of condition will be made constantly and with growing loudness till it *must* be listened to, and then at last it will only be a step over the border, and the civilized world will be socialized; and, looking back on what has been, we shall be astonished to think of how long we submitted to live as we live now.

. . . There was no sign of revolutionary feeling in England twenty years ago: the middle class were so rich that they had no need to hope for anything—but a heaven which they did not believe in: the well-to-do working men did not hope, since they were not pinched and had no means of learning their degraded position: and lastly, the drudges of the proletariat had such hope as charity, the hospital, the workhouse, and kind death at last could offer them.

In this stock-jobbers' heaven let us leave our dear countrymen for a little, while I say a few words about the affairs of the people on the continent of Europe. Things were not quite so smooth for the fleecer there: Socialist thinkers and writers had arisen about the same time as Robert Owen; St. Simon, Proudhon, Fourier and his followers kept up the traditions of hope in the midst of a *bourgeois* world.

. . . Now, in all I have been saying, I have been wanting you to trace the fact that, ever since the establishment of commercialism on the ruins of feudality, there has been growing a steady feeling on the part of the workers that they are a class dealt with as a class, and in like manner to deal with others; and that as this class feeling has grown, so also has grown with it a consciousness of the antagonism between their class and the class which employs it, as the phrase goes; that is to say, which lives by means of its labour.

Now it is just this growing consciousness of the fact that as long as there exists in society a propertied class living on the labour of a propertyless one, there *must* be a struggle always going on between these two classes—it is just the dawning knowledge of this fact which should show us what civilization can hope for—namely, transformation into true society, in which there will no longer be classes with their necessary struggle for existence and superiority: for the antagonism of classes which began in all simplicity between the master and the chattel slave of ancient society, and was continued between the feudal lord and the serf of mediaeval society, has gradually become the contention between the capitalist developed from the workmen of the last-named period, and the wage-earner:. . . .

. . . Moreover, the capitalist or modern slave-owner has been forced by his very success, as we have seen, to organize his slaves, the wage-earners, into a co-operation for production so well arranged that it requires little but his own elimination to make it a foundation for communal life: in the teeth also of the experience of past ages, he has been compelled to allow a modicum of education to the propertyless, and has not even been able to deprive them wholly of political rights; his own advance in wealth and power has bred for him the very enemy who is doomed to make an end of him.

But will there be any new class to take the place of the present proletariat when that has triumphed, as it must do, over the present privileged class? We cannot foresee the future, but we may fairly hope not: at least we cannot see any signs of such a new class forming. It is impossible to see how destruction of privilege can stop short of absolute equality of condition; pure Communism is the logical deduction from the imperfect form of the new society, which is generally differentiated from it as Socialism.

Meantime, it is this simplicity and directness of the growing contest which above all things presents itself as a terror to the conservative instinct of the present day. Many among the middle class who are sincerely grieved and shocked at the condition of the proletariat which civilization has created, and even alarmed by the frightful inequalities which it fosters, do nevertheless shudder back from the idea of the class struggle, and strive to shut their eyes to the fact that it is going on. They try to think that peace is not only possible, but natural, between the two classes, the very essence of whose existence is that each can only thrive by what it manages to force the other to yield to it. They propose to themselves the impossible problem of raising the inferior or exploited classes into a position in which they will cease to struggle against the superior classes, while the latter will not cease to exploit them. This absurd position drives them into the concoction of schemes for bettering the condition of the working classes at their own expense, some of them futile, some merely fantastic; or they may be divided again into those which point out the advantages and pleasures of involuntary asceticism, and reactionary plans for importing the conditions of the production and life of the Middle Ages (wholly misunderstood by them, by the way) into the present system of the capitalist farmer, the great industries, and the universal world-market. Some see a solution of the social problem in sham co-operation, which is merely an improved form of joint-stockery: others preach thrift to (precarious) incomes of eighteen shillings a week, and industry to men killing themselves by inches in working overtime or to men whom the labour-market has rejected as not wanted: others beg the proletarians not to breed so fast; an injunction the compliance with which might be at first of advantage to the proletarians themselves in their present condition, but would certainly undo the capitalists, if it were carried to any lengths, and would lead through ruin and misery to the violent outbreak of the very revolution which these timid people are so anxious to forego.

... The greater part of these schemes aim, though seldom with the con-sciousness of their promoters, at the creation of a new middle-class out of the wage-earning class, and at their expense, just as the present middle-class was developed out of the serf-population of the early Middle Ages. It may be pos-sible that such a *further* development of the middle-class lies before us, but it will not be brought about by any such artificial means as the above-mentioned schemes. If it comes at all, it must be produced by events, which at present we cannot foresee, acting on our commercial system, and revivifying for a little time, maybe, that Capitalist Society which now seems sickening towards its end.

For what is visible before us in these days is the competitive commercial system killing itself by its own force: profits lessening, businesses growing bigger and bigger, the small employer of labour thrust out of his function, and the aggregation of capital increasing the numbers of the lower middle-class from above rather than from below, by driving the smaller manufacturer into the position of a mere servant to the bigger. The productivity of labour also increasing out of all proportion to the capacity of the capitalists to manage the market or deal with the labour supply: lack of employment therefore becoming chronic, and discontent therewithal.

All this on the one hand. On the other, the workman claiming everywhere political equality, which cannot long be denied; and education spreading, so that what between the improvement in the education of the working-class and the continued amazing fatuity of that of the upper classes, there is a distinct tendency to equalization here; and, as I have hinted above, all history shows us what a danger to society may be a class at once educated and socially degraded: though, indeed, no history has yet shown us—what is swiftly advancing upon us—a class which, though it shall have attained knowledge, shall lack utterly the refinement and self-respect which come from the union of knowledge with leisure and ease of life. The growth of such a class may well make the "cultured" people of to-day tremble.

Whatever, therefore, of unforeseen and unconceived-of may lie in the womb of the future, there is nothing visible before us but a decaying system, with no outlook but ever-increasing entanglement and blindness, and a new system, Socialism, the hope of which is ever growing clearer in men's minds—a system which not only sees how labour can be freed from its present fetters, and organized unwastefully, so as to produce the greatest possible amount of wealth for the community and for every member of it, but which bears with it its own ethics and religion and aesthetics: that is the hope and promise of a new and higher life in all ways. So that even if those unforeseen economical events above spoken of were to happen, and put off for a while the end of our Capitalist system, the latter would drag itself along as an anomaly cursed by all, a mere clog on the aspirations of humanity.

It is not likely that it will come to that: in all probability the logical outcome of the latter days of Capitalism will go step by step with its actual history: while all men, even its declared enemies, will be working to bring Socialism about, the aims of those who have learned to believe in the certainty and beneficence of its advent will become clearer, their methods for realizing it clearer also, and at last ready to hand. Then will come that open acknowledgment for the necessity of the change (an acknowledgment coming from the intelligence of civilization) which is commonly called Revolution. It is no use prophesying as to the events which will accompany that revolution, but to a reasonable man it seems unlikely to the last degree, or we will say impossible, that a moral sentiment will induce the proprietary classes—those who live by *owning* the means of production which the unprivileged classes must needs *use*—to yield up this privilege uncompelled; all one can hope is that they will see the implicit threat of compulsion in the events of the day, and so yield with a good grace to the terrible necessity of forming part of a world in which all, including themselves, will work honestly and live easily.

# peter kropotkin

Prince Peter Kropotkin was a Russian geographer and revolutionary whose un-worldly demeanor and cheerful endurance of hardships endeared him to leaders of the anarchist movement which he supported. Born in Moscow, the son of Prince Aleksei Petrovich Kropotkin, he was educated at the School of Pages in St. Petersburg and was later appointed to the personal suite of Czar Alexander II. The tedious formalities of court life not only disappointed his expectations but also undermined his early impressions of the Czar who had emancipated Russia's serfs. The intimacy of court life revealed the Czar to be a capricious and vindictive man. Much to the dismay of his ambitious relatives, Kropotkin ef-fected an escape from the Court by accepting a commission with the Amur Kossack cavalry regiment. While serving five years with the regiment in Siberia, during which time he lost all faith in government-imposed discipline, he de-veloped his interest in wildlife and geological phenomena; he also made some scientifically important discoveries about the structural lines of the main moun-tain ranges of eastern Asia.

Traveling to Switzerland in 1872, Kropotkin met the noted anarchist Mikhail Bakunin and lived with the watchmakers of the Jura federation. The watch-makers' friendly, industrious, and efficient guilds made a significant impression upon him, and Kropotkin concluded that they were a model of disciplined and happy anarchy, a shining example of how the peoples of the world could achieve practical social cooperation without oppressive state controls. Upon his return to Russia, he joined an activist group of social reformers, but in 1873 he was arrested and imprisoned for "seditious" propaganda. Kropotkin, whose desire to identify with the poor had led him to discontinue the use of his title, escaped two years later and made his way to France. When he was next arrested in that country, Georges Clemenceau and other friends secured him a pardon. He lived most of his remaining years in England, visiting the United States twice, where he gave addresses at Wellesley College and at Harvard University.

Viewing the nineteenth century nation-state as a repressive superstructure which had long since outgrown its original usefulness, Kropotkin expected that voluntary societies would gradually inherit and transform the system. He welcomed World War I because he believed that it would destroy, once and for all, the obsolete military powers which had provoked it. In 1917 he rejoiced at the March revolution in Russia and hastened back to his native land. Long idolized by the workers in France, and regarded with esteem in both Britain and America, Kropotkin did not find similar tolerance among some revolutionaries in his own country because his opposition to Bolshevism was fundamental and unconcealed. He called the followers of Lenin "aliens, enemies of Russia, gangsters," who had betrayed the revolution. He lamented that, instead of setting Russia on the path leading toward voluntary federation, the alleged Communists (who never practiced communism, but only national state socialism) would only succeed in making people hate their very name. Yet he vehemently denounced the western Allies' intervention in the Russian civil war.

Reduced to silent inactivity while the civil war was raging, Kropotkin died on February 8, 1921, at Dmitrov, forty miles from Moscow. The family, respecting his principles, declined the offer of a state funeral. The government chose to overlook the earlier criticisms of the popular Kropotkin; it made his birthplace a museum to contain his books and other suitable collections, and gave his name to a street in Moscow.

People who had remained unswayed by Bakunin's spell and resentful of the bomb-throwing that it inspired in earlier anarchists were fascinated by Kropotkin's personality, despite the naivete of some of his political ideas. He brought respectability to the anarchist movement, and his mellow humaneness and personal warmth had a strong appeal, especially in France and England. His major writings were produced between 1885 and 1904; one of his more significant works, *La conquête du pain* ("The Conquest of Bread"), appeared first in 1892 and perhaps best reveals the thinking and the humanity of this aristocrat of the people.

## On Communistic Anarchy

... In our civilized societies we are rich. Why then are the many poor? Why this painful drudgery for the masses? Why, even to the best paid workman, this uncertainty for the morrow, in the midst of all the wealth inherited from the past, and in spite of the powerful means of production, which could ensure comfort to all, in return for a few hours of daily toil?

The Socialists have said it and repeated it unwearyingly. Daily they reiterate it, demonstrating it by arguments taken from all the sciences. It is because all that is necessary for production—the land, the mines, the highways, machinery, food, shelter, education, knowledge—all have been seized by the few in the course of that long story of robbery, enforced migration and wars, of ignorance and oppression, which has been the life of the human race before it had learned to subdue the forces of Nature. It is because, taking advantage of alleged rights acquired in the past, these few appropriate to-day two-thirds of the products of human labour, and then squander them in the most stupid and shameful way. It is because, having reduced the masses to a point at which they have not the means of subsistence for a month, or even for a week in advance, the few can allow the many to work, only on the condition of themselves receiving the lion's share. It is because these few prevent the remainder of men from producing the things they need, and force them to produce, not the necessaries of life for all, but whatever offers the greatest profits to the monopolists.

... Fine sermons have been preached on the text that those who have should share with those who have not, but he who would carry out this principle would be speedily informed that these beautiful sentiments are all very well in poetry, but not in practice. "To lie is to degrade and besmirch oneself," we say, and yet all civilized life becomes one huge lie. We accustom ourselves and our children to hypocrisy, to the practice of a double-faced morality. And since the brain is ill at ease among lies, we cheat ourselves with sophistry. Hypocrisy and sophistry become the second nature of the civilized man.

But a society cannot live thus; it must return to truth, or cease to exist.

Thus the consequences which spring from the original act of monopoly spread through the whole of social life. Under the pain of death, human societies are forced to return to first principles: the means of production being the collective work of humanity, the product should be the collective property of the race. Individual appropriation is neither just nor serviceable. All belongs to all. All things are for all men, since all men have need of them, since all men have

From Peter Kropotkin, *The Conquest of Bread*, Vanguard Press, New York, 1906, pp. 3, 10-11, 16-17, 19-23, 28-30, 32, 41-42, 44, 46, 49-50, 62-64, 167, 209-212.

worked in the measure of their strength to produce them, and since it is not possible to evaluate every one's part in the production of the world's wealth.

... All is for all! If the man and the woman bear their fair share of work, they have a right to their fair share of all that is produced by all, and that share is enough to secure them well-being. No more of such vague formulas as "The right to work," or "To each the whole result of his labour." What we proclaim is THE RIGHT TO WELL-BEING: WELL-BEING FOR ALL!

... But, if plenty for all is to become a reality, this immense capital—cities, houses, pastures, arable lands, factories, highways, education—must cease to be regarded as private property, for the monopolist to dispose of at his pleasure.

This rich endowment, painfully won, builded, fashioned or invented by our ancestors, must become common property so that the collective interests of men may gain from it the greatest good for all.

There must be EXPROPRIATION. The well-being of all—the end; expropriation—the means.

EXPROPRIATION, such then is the problem which History has put before the men of the twentieth century; the return to Communism in all that ministers to the well-being of man.

But this problem cannot be solved by means of legislation. No one imagines that. The poor, as well as the rich, understand that neither the existing Governments, nor any which might arise out of possible political changes, would be capable of finding such a solution. They feel the necessity of a social revolution; and both rich and poor recognize that this revolution is imminent, that it may break out in a few years.

... Whence will the revolution come? how will it announce its coming? No one can answer these questions. The future is hidden. But those who watch and think do not misinterpret the signs: workers and exploiters, Revolutionists and Conservatives, thinkers and men of action, all feel that a revolution is at our doors.

Well, then,—What are we going to do when the thunderbolt has fallen?

We have all been bent on studying the dramatic side of revolutions so much, and the practical work of revolutions so little, that we are apt to see only the stage effects, so to speak, of these great movements; the fight of the first days; the barricades. But this fight, this first skirmish, is soon ended, and it is only after the breakdown of the old system that the real work of revolution can be said to begin.

... All this may please those who like the stage, but it is not revolution. Nothing has been accomplished as yet.

And meanwhile the people suffer. The factories are idle, the workshops closed; trade is at a standstill. The worker does not even earn the meagre wage which was his before. Food goes up in price. With that heroic devotion which has always characterized them, and which in great crises reaches the sublime, the people will wait patiently.

. . . The people . . . . suffer and say: "How is a way out of these difficulties to be found?"

It seems to us that there is only one answer to this question: We must recognize, and loudly proclaim, that every one, whatever his grade in the old society, whether strong or weak, capable or incapable, has, before everything, THE RIGHT TO LIVE and that society is bound to share amongst all, without exception, the means of existence it has at its disposal. We must acknowledge this, and proclaim it aloud, and act up to it.

Affairs must be managed in such a way that from the first day of the revolution the worker shall know that a new era is opening before him; that henceforward none need crouch under the bridges, while palaces are hard by, none need fast in the midst of plenty, none need perish with cold near shops full of furs; that all is for all, in practice as well as in theory, and that at last, for the first time in history, a revolution has been accomplished which considers the NEEDS of the people before schooling them in their DUTIES.

This cannot be brought about by Acts of Parliament, but only by taking immediate and effective possession of all that is necessary to ensure the well-being of all; this is the only really scientific way of going to work, the only way which can be understood and desired by the mass of the people. We must take possession, in the name of the people, of the granaries, the shops full of clothing and the dwelling houses. Nothing must be wasted. We must organize without delay a way to feed the hungry, to satisfy all wants, to meet all needs, to produce not for the special benefit of this one or that one, but so as to ensure to society as a whole its life and further development.

Enough of ambiguous words like "the right to work," with which the people were misled in 1848, and which are still resorted to with the hope of misleading them. Let us have the courage to recognise that *Well-being for all,* henceforward possible, must be realized.

. . . The "right to well-being" means the possibility of living like human beings, and of bringing up children to be members of a society better than ours, whilst the "right to work" only means the right to be always a wage-slave, a drudge, ruled over and exploited by the middle class of the future. The right to well-being is the Social Revolution, the right to work means nothing but the Treadmill of Commercialism. It is high time for the worker to assert his right to the common inheritance, and to enter into possession of it.

Every society, on abolishing private property, will be forced, we maintain, to organize itself on the lines of Communistic Anarchy. Anarchy leads to Communism, and Communism to Anarchy, both alike being expressions of the predominant tendency in modern societies, the pursuit of equality.

... But ours is neither the Communism of Fourier ... nor of the German State Socialists. It is Anarchist Communism, Communism without government—the Communism of the Free. It is the synthesis of the two ideals pursued by humanity throughout the ages—Economic and Political Liberty.

In taking "Anarchy" for our ideal of political organization we are only giving expression to another marked tendency of human progress. Whenever European societies have developed up to a certain point, they have shaken off the yoke of authority and substituted a system founded more or less on the principles of individual liberty. And history shows us that these periods of partial or general revolution, when the old governments were overthrown, were also periods of sudden progress both in the economic and the intellectual field. So it was after the enfranchisement of the communes, whose monuments, produced by the free labour of the guilds, have never been surpassed; so it was after the great peasant uprising which brought about the Reformation and imperilled the papacy; and so it was again with the society, free for a brief space, which was created on the other side of the Atlantic by the malcontents from the Old World.

And, if we observe the present development of civilized nations, we see, most unmistakably, a movement ever more and more marked tending to limit the sphere of action of the Government, and to allow more and more liberty to the individual. This evolution is going on before our eyes, though cumbered by the ruins and rubbish of old institutions and old superstitions. Like all evolutions, it only waits a revolution to overthrow the old obstacles which block the way, that it may find free scope in a regenerated society.

After having striven long in vain to solve the insoluble problem—the problem of constructing a government "which will constrain the individual to obedience without itself ceasing to be the servant of society," men at last attempt to free themselves from every form of government and to satisfy their need for organization by free contacts between individuals and groups pursuing the same aim. The independence of each small territorial unit becomes a pressing need; mutual agreement replaces law in order to regulate individual interests in view of a common object—very often disregarding the frontiers of the present States.

All that was once looked on as a function of the Government is to-day called in question. Things are arranged more easily and more satisfactorily without the intervention of the State. And in studying the progress made in this direction, we are led to conclude that the tendency of the human race is to reduce Government interference to zero; in fact, to abolish the State, the personification of injustice, oppression, and monopoly.

We can already catch glimpses of a world in which the bonds which bind the individual are no longer laws, but social habits—the result of the need felt by each one of us to seek the support, the co-operation, the sympathy of his neighbours.

Assuredly the idea of a society without a State will give rise to at least as many objections as the political economy of a society without private capital. We have all been brought up from our childhood to regard the State as a sort of Providence; all our education, the Roman history we learned at school, the Byzantine code which we studied later under the name of Roman law, and the various sciences taught at the universities, accustom us to believe in Government and in the virtues of the State providential.

To maintain this superstition whole systems of philosophy have been elaborated and taught; all politics are based on this principle; and each politician, whatever his colours, comes forward and says to the people, "Give my party the power; we can and we will free you from the miseries which press so heavily upon you."

From the cradle to the grave all our actions are guided by this principle. Open any book on sociology or jurisprudence, and you will find there the Government, its organization, its acts, filling so large a place that we come to believe that there is nothing outside the Government and the world of statesmen.

. . . The history of the last fifty years furnishes a living proof that Representative Government is impotent to discharge all the functions we have sought to assign to it. In days to come the nineteenth century will be quoted as having witnessed the failure of parliamentarianism.

This impotence is becoming so evident to all; the faults of parliamentarianism, and the inherent vices of the representative principle, are so self-evident, that the few thinkers who have made a critical study of them (J. S. Mill, Leverdays), did but give literary form to the popular dissatisfaction. It is not difficult, indeed, to see the absurdity of naming a few men and saying to them, "Make laws regulating all our spheres of activity, although not one of you knows anything about them!"

We are beginning to see that government by majorities means abandoning all the affairs of the country to the tide-waiters who make up the majorities in the House and in election committees; to those, in a word, who have no opinion of their own.

. . . The ideas of Anarchism in general and of Expropriation in particular find much more sympathy than we are apt to imagine among men of independent character, and those for whom idleness is not the supreme ideal. "Still," our friends often warn us, "take care you do not go too far! Humanity cannot be changed in a day, so do not be in too great a hurry with your schemes of Expropriation and Anarchy, or you will be in danger of achieving no permanent result."

Now, what we fear with regard to Expropriation is exactly the contrary. We are afraid of not going far enough, of carrying out Expropriation on too small a scale to be lasting. We would not have the revolutionary impulse arrested in mid-career, to exhaust itself in half measures, which would content no one, and while producing a tremendous confusion in society, and stopping its customary activities, would have no vital power—would merely spread general discontent and inevitably prepare the way for the triumph of reaction.

. . . All is interdependent in a civilized society; it is impossible to reform any one thing without altering the whole. Therefore, on the day a nation will strike at private property, under any one of its forms, territorial or industrial, it will be obliged to attack them all. The very success of the Revolution will impose it.

Besides, even if it were desired, it would be impossible to confine the change to a partial expropriation. Once the principle of the "Divine Right of Property" is shaken, no amount of theorizing will prevent its overthrow, here by the slaves of the field, there by the slaves of the machine.

. . . Whether we like it or not, this is what the people mean by a revolution. As soon as they have made a clean sweep of the Government, they will seek first of all to ensure to themselves decent dwellings and sufficient food and clothes—free of capitalist rent.

And the people will be right. The methods of the people will be much more in accordance with science than those of the economists who draw so many distinctions between instruments of production and articles of consumption. The people understand that this is just the point where the Revolution ought to begin; and they will lay the foundations of the only economic science worthy the name—a science which might be called: "*The Study of the Needs of Humanity, and of the Economic Means to satisfy them.*"

. . . "Bread, it is bread that the Revolution needs!"

Let others spend their time in issuing pompous proclamations, in decorating themselves lavishly with official gold lace, and in talking about political liberty! . . .

Be it ours to see, from the first day of the Revolution to the last, in all the provinces fighting for freedom, that there is not a single man who lacks bread, not a single woman compelled to stand with the wearied crowd outside the bakehousedoor, that haply a coarse loaf may be thrown to her in charity, not a single child pining for want of food.

... We have the temerity to declare that all have a right to bread, that there is bread enough for all, and that with this watchword of *Bread for All* the Revolution will triumph.

That we are Utopians is well known. So Utopian are we that we go the length of believing that the Revolution can and ought to assure shelter, food, and clothes to all—an idea extremely displeasing to middle-class citizens, whatever their party colour, for they are quite alive to the fact that it is not easy to keep the upper hand of a people whose hunger is satisfied.

All the same, we maintain our contention: bread must be found for the people of the Revolution, and the question of bread must take precedence of all other questions. If it is settled in the interests of the people, the Revolution will be on the right road; for in solving the question of Bread we must accept the principle of equality, which will force itself upon us to the exclusion of every other solution.

... If the entire nation, or, better still, if all Europe should accomplish the Social Revolution simultaneously, and start with thorough-going Communism, our procedure would be simplified; but if only a few communities in Europe make the attempt, other means will have to be chosen. The circumstances will dictate the measures.

We are thus led, before we proceed further, to glance at the State of Europe, and, without pretending to prophesy, we may try to foresee what course the Revolution will take, or at least what will be its essential features.

Certainly it would be very desirable that all Europe should rise at once, that expropriation should be general, and that communistic principles should inspire all and sundry. Such a universal rising would do much to simplify the task of our century.

But all the signs lead us to believe that it will not take place. That the Revolution will embrace Europe we do not doubt....But whether the Revolution would everywhere exhibit the same characteristics is highly doubtful.

It is more than probable that expropriation will be everywhere carried into effect on a larger scale, and that this policy carried out by any one of the great nations of Europe will influence all the rest; yet the beginnings of the Revolution will exhibit great local differences, and its course will vary in different countries.

... Will it therefore be necessary, as is sometimes suggested, that the nations in the vanguard of the movement should adapt their pace to those who lag behind? Must we wait till the Communist Revolution is ripe in all civilized countries? Clearly not! Even if it were a thing to be desired, it is not possible. History does not wait for the laggards.

... the day on which old institutions will fall under the proletarian axe, voices will cry out: "Bread, shelter, ease for all!" And those voices will be listened to; the people will say: "Let us begin by allaying our thirst for life, for happiness, for liberty, that we have never quenched. And when we shall have tasted of this joy, we will set to work to demolish the last vestiges of middle-class rule; its morality drawn from account books, its 'debit and credit' philosophy, its 'mine and your' institutions. 'In demolishing we shall build,' as Proudhon said; and we shall build in the name of Communism and Anarchy."

... We can easily perceive the new horizons opening before the social revolution.

... At what, then, should the hundreds of thousands of workers, who are asphyxiated to-day in small workshops and factories, be employed on the day they regain their liberty? Will they continue to shut themselves up in factories after the Revolution? Will they continue to make luxurious toys for export when they see their stock or corn getting exhausted, meat becoming scarce, and vegetables disappearing without being replaced?

Evidently not! They will leave the town and go into the fields! Aided by a machinery which will enable the weakest of us to put a shoulder to the wheel, they will carry revolution into previously enslaved culture as they will have carried it into institutions and ideas.

... And in two or three months the early crops will receive the most pressing wants, and provide food for a people who, after so many centuries of expectation, will at least be able to appease their hunger and eat according to their appetite.

... The only thing that may be wanting to the Revolution is the boldness of initiative.

With our minds already narrowed in our youth and enslaved by the past in our mature age, we hardly dare to think. If a new idea is mentioned—before venturing on an opinion of our own, we consult musty books a hundred years old, to know what ancient masters thought on the subject.

It is not food that will fail, if boldness of thought and initiative are not wanting to the revolution.

... it will ... be by the working in common of the soil that the enfranchised societies will find their unity and will obliterate the hatred and oppression which has hitherto divided them.

Henceforth, able to conceive solidarity—that immense power which increases man's energy and creative forces a hundredfold—the new society will march to the conquest of the future with all the vigour of youth.

Ceasing to produce for unknown buyers, and looking in its midst for needs and tastes to be satisfied, society will liberally assure the life and ease of each of its members, as well as the moral satisfaction which work gives when freely chosen and freely accomplished, and the joy of living without encroaching on the life of others.

Inspired by a new daring—born of the feeling of solidarity—all will march together to the conquest of the high joys of knowledge and artistic creation.

A society thus inspired will fear neither dissensions within nor enemies without. To the coalitions of the past it will oppose a new harmony, the initiative of each and all, the daring which springs from the awakening of a people's genius.

Before such an irresistible force "conspiring kings" will be powerless. Nothing will remain for them but to bow before it, and to harness themselves to the chariot of humanity, rolling towards new horizons opened up by the Social Revolution.

# georges sorel

Georges Sorel was a civil engineer by profession, but his interests in contemporary social problems prompted him to resign his position and devote his energies to study and writing. Sorel, who was born in Cherbourg, France, on November 2, 1847, always retained a lively interest in the philosophies of science and technology as evidenced by his several publications on the subject. He is best remembered, however, as a French social philosopher and as an unorthodox commentator on Marxism.

Sorel was intensely critical of the French Third Republic in particular, and democracy in general, and he became increasingly interested in socialist thought. Finding in the political and social life of democracy the triumph of mediocrity, Sorel espoused various forms of socialism which led him gradually to syndicalism. The latter embraced a plan for reorganizing society and a strategy for revolutionary action for the overthrow of the state. Like anarchists, syndicalists believed that any form of state is an instrument of oppression and that all states should be abolished. They stressed the function of productive labor and regarded the trade union as the essential unit of production and of government. In motive, the work of the unions would be socialistic—for use, not for profit. The general strike, sabotage, slowdowns, and other means of disrupting ordinary production were advocated by some syndicalists as a means of assuming control of the manufacturing process, seen as essential to their aims.

Syndicalist doctrine was substantially influenced by the writings of Pierre Proudhon, with his attacks on property, and of Georges Sorel, who espoused violence. Syndicalism, like anarchism, flourished largely in Latin countries, especially in France, where trade unionism was for years strongly influenced by syndicalist programs. In the United States the chief organization of the syndicalist type was the Industrial Workers of the World, which flourished early in the twentieth century but was virtually extinguished after the First World War by government suppression and internal rifts.

After resigning as a civil engineer, Sorel devoted much of his time to writing articles for various French and Italian periodicals, but his writings were unsystematic and of uneven quality. Originally he had been a liberal conservative, as can be seen from his *Procès de Socrate* (1889), but in 1893 he discovered Marxism and began writing the analytical critiques that number among his most original and valuable achievements. He strongly opposed Karl Kautsky's determinist simplifications and viewed Marxism as a philosophy of freedom and action. By 1902 his thought had grown more extreme, and he enthusiastically supported revolutionary syndicalism, which focused upon the spontaneity of the class struggle. His most famous work *Réflexions sur la violence* [Reflections on Violence] was published in 1908 and represents in many ways the high point in the development of his philosophical thinking.

After 1909 Sorel's thought took a less certain direction. Feeling obliged to revise his revolutionary syndicalism, he drifted, not without strong misgivings, toward the monarchist movement Action francaise. But he changed again in 1914, judging World War I to be a betrayal, and he eventually declared himself for Bolshevism in 1919—with the more enthusiasm because he truly believed it to be a lost cause. He died at Boulogne-sur-Seine on August 28, 1922.

Sorel is sometimes held to have inspired both Communist and Fascist dictatorships, but his influence on either is difficult to demonstrate. Lenin had only contempt for him since Sorel denounced everything that might subject socialist action to control by party leaders. Benito Mussolini, however, frequently professed himself to be a disciple of Sorel, whose theories of "myth" and of "violence" he took to glorify the blind motivation of the mob and to justify mere physical brutality—distortions which Sorel explicitly condemned.

Georges Sorel is receiving new attention today as both activists and political theorists explore classic writings on revolution and violence. One example of the renewed interest in Sorel is Irving Louis Horowitz's excellent study *Radicalism and the Revolt against Reason,* the 1968 edition of which examines the relation between the social theories of Georges Sorel and American thought in the 1960's.

The selection which follows was excerpted from Sorel's *Reflections on Vio-*

*lence.* In it he developed his notions of "force" and of "violence." Violence for Sorel was the revolutionary denial of the existing order; but in describing its creative historical role he opposed it to "force," that is, to the state's power of coercion, the abuse of which he consistently denounced. In the concluding appendix, here included, entitled "Apology for Violence," Sorel displays an intense bitterness toward Jean Juarès, the French socialist leader and historian. Juarès believed economic equality would come as the result of peaceful revolution, an idealism which was viewed as utopian by most socialists. Marxists, anarchists, and syndicalists like Sorel, who were apostles of force and violence, regarded such thinking with contempt.

## On Violence and Revolutionary Syndicalism

...To examine the effects of violence it is necessary to start from its distant consequences and not from its immediate results. We should not ask whether it is more or less directly advantageous for contemporary workmen than adroit diplomacy would be, but we should inquire what will result from the introduction of violence into the relations of the proletariat with society. We are not comparing two kinds of reformism, but we are endeavouring to find out what contemporary violence is in relation to the future social revolution.

... the most decisive factor in social politics is the cowardice of the Government. This was shown in the plainest possible way in the recent discussions on the suppression of registry offices, and on the law which sent to the civil courts appeals against the decisions of the arbitrators in industrial disputes. Nearly all the Syndicalist leaders know how to make excellent use of this situation, and they teach the workers that it is not at all a question of demanding favours, but that they must profit by *middle-class cowardice* to impose the will of the proletariat. These tactics are supported by so many facts that they were bound to take root in the working class world.

One of the things which appear to me to have most astonished the workers during the last few years has been the timidity of the forces of law and order in the presence of a riot; magistrates who have the right to demand the services of soldiers dare not use their power to the utmost, and officers allow themselves to be abused and struck with a patience hitherto unknown in them. It is becoming

From Georges Sorel, *Reflections on Violence*, translated by T.E. Hulme, Peter Smith, New York, 1941, pp. 47-48, 69-73, 84-91, 98-99, 121-122, 186-187, 297-299.

more and more evident every day that working-class violence possesses an extraordinary efficacy in strikes: prefects, fearing that they may be obliged to use force against insurrectionary violence, bring pressure to bear on employers in order to compel them to give way; the safety of factories is now looked upon as a favour which the prefect may dispense as he pleases; consequently he arranges the use of his police so as to intimidate the two parties, and skilfully brings them to an agreement.

Trades union leaders have not been long in grasping the full bearing of this situation, and it must be admitted that they have used the weapon that has been put into their hands with great skill. They endeavour to intimidate the prefects by popular demonstrations which might lead to serious conflicts with the police, and they commend violence as the most efficacious means of obtaining concessions. At the end of a certain time and obsessed and frightened administration nearly always intervenes with the masters and forces an agreement upon them, which becomes an encouragement to the propagandists of violence.

Whether we approve or condemn what is called *the revolutionary and direct method,* it is evident that it is not on the point of disappearing; in a country as warlike as France there are profound reasons which would assure a considerable popularity for this method, even if its enormous efficacy had not been demonstrated by so many examples. This is the one great social fact of the present hour, and we must seek to understand its bearing.

I cannot refrain from noting down here a reflection made by Clemenceau with regard to our relations with Germany, which applies equally well to social conflicts when they take a violent aspect (which seems likely to become more and more general in proportion as a cowardly middle class continues to pursue the chimera of social peace): "There is no better means," he said (than the policy of perpetual concessions), "of making the opposite party ask for more and more. Every man or every power whose action consists solely in surrender can only finish by self-annihilation. Everything that lives resists; that which does not resist allows itself to be cut up piecemeal" (*Aurore,* August 15, 1905).

A social policy founded on middle-class cowardice, which consists in always surrendering before the threat of violence, cannot fail to engender the idea that the middle class is condemned to death, and that its disappearance is only a matter of time. Thus every conflict which gives rise to violence becomes a vanguard fight, and nobody can foresee what will arise from such engagements; although the great battle never comes to a head, yet each time they come to blows the strikers hope that it is the beginning of the great *Napoleonic battle* (that which will definitely crush the vanquished); in this way the practice of strikes engenders the notion of a catastrophic revolution.

A keen observer of the contemporary proletarian movement has expressed the same ideas: "They, like their ancestors (the French revolutionaries), are for struggle, for conquest; they desire to accomplish great works by force. Only, the war of conquest interests them no longer. Instead of thinking of battles, they now think of strikes; instead of setting up as their ideal a battle against the armies of Europe, they now set up the general strike in which the capitalist regime will be annihilated."

The theorists of social peace shut their eyes to these embarrassing facts; they are doubtless ashamed to admit their cowardice, just as the Government is ashamed to admit that its social politics are carried out under the threat of disturbances. It is curious that people who boast of having read Le Play have not observed that his conception of the conditions of social peace was quite different from that of his imbecile successors. He supposed the existence of a middle class of serious moral habits, imbued with the feelings of its own dignity, and having the energy necessary to govern the country without recourse to the old traditional bureaucracy. To those men, who held riches and power in their hands, he professed to teach their *social duty towards their subjects.* His system supposed an undisputed authority; it is well known that he deplored the licence of the press under Napoleon III as scandalous and dangerous; his reflections on this subject seem somewhat ludicrous to those who compare the newspaper of that time with those of to-day. Nobody in his time would have believed that a great country would accept peace at any price; his point of view in this matter did not differ greatly from that of Clemenceau. He would never have admitted that any one could be cowardly and hypocritical enough to decorate with the name of social duty the cowardice of a middle class incapable of defending itself.

Middle-class cowardice very much resembles the cowardice of the English Liberal party, which constantly proclaims its absolute confidence in arbitration between nations: arbitration nearly always gives disastrous results for England. But these *worthy progressives* prefer to pay, or even to compromise the future of their country, rather than face the horrors of war. The English Liberal party has the word *justice* always on its lips, absolutely like our middle class; we might very well wonder whether all the high morality of our great contemporary thinkers is not founded on a degradation of the sentiment of honour.

. . . According to Marx, capitalism, by reason of the innate laws of its own nature, is hurrying along a path which will lead the world of to-day, with the inevitability of the evolution of organic life, to the doors of the world of to-morrow. This movement comprises a long period of capitalistic construction, and it ends by a rapid destruction, which is the work of the proletariat. Capitalism creates the heritage which Socialism will receive, the men who will suppress the present regime, and the means of bringing about this destruction, at the same time that it preserves the results obtained in production. Capitalism begets new ways of working; it throws the working class into revolutionary organisations by the pressure it exercises on wages; it restricts its own political basis by competition, which is constantly eliminating industrial leaders. Thus, after having solved the great problem of the organisation of labour, to effect which Utopians have brought forward so many naive or stupid hypotheses, capitalism provokes the birth of the cause which will overthrow it, and thus renders useless everything that Utopians have written to induce enlightened people to make reforms; and it gradually ruins the traditional order, against which the critics of the idealists had proved themselves to be so deplorably incompetent. . . . Without any co-ordinated plan, without any directive ideas, without any ideal of a future world, it is the cause of an inevitable evolution; it draws from the present all that the present can give towards historical development; it performs in an almost mechanical manner all that is necessary, in order that a new era may appear, and that this new era may break every link with the idealism of the present times, while preserving the acquisitions of the capitalistic economic system.

Socialists should therefore abandon the attempt (initiated by the Utopians) to find a means of inducing the enlightened middle class to prepare the *transition to a more perfect system of legislation*; their sole function is that of explaining to the proletariat the greatness of the revolutionary part they are called upon to play. By ceaseless criticism, the proletariat must be brought to perfect their organisations; they must be shown how the embryonic forms which appear in their unions may be developed so that, finally, they may build up institutions without any parallel in the history of the middle class; that they may form ideas which depend solely on their position as producers in large industries, and which owe nothing to middle-class thought; and that they may acquire *habits of liberty* with which the middle class nowadays are no longer acquainted.

This doctrine will evidently be inapplicable if the middle class and the proletariat do not oppose each other implacably, with all the forces at their disposal; the more ardently capitalist the middle class is, the more the proletariat is full of a warlike spirit and confident of its revolutionary strength, the more certain will be the success of the proletarian movement.

The middle class with which Marx was familiar in England was still, as regards the immense majority, animated by their conquering, insatiable, and pitiless spirit, which had characterised at the beginning of modern times the creators of new industries and the adventurers launched on the discovery of unknown lands. When we are studying the modern industrial system we should always bear in mind this similarity between the capitalist type and the warrior type; it was for very good reasons that the men who directed gigantic enterprises were named *captains of industry.* This type is still found to-day in all its purity in the United States: there are found the indomitable energy, the audacity based on a just appreciation of its strength, the cold calculation of interests, which are the qualities of great generals and great capitalists. According to Paul de Rousiers, every American feels himself capable of "trying his luck" on the battlefield of business, so that the general spirit of the country is in complete harmony with that of the multimillionaires; our men of letters are exceedingly surprised to see these latter condemning themselves to lead to the end of their days a galley-slave existence, without ever thinking of leading a nobleman's life for themselves, as the Rothschilds do.

In a society so enfevered by the passion for the success which can be obtained in competition, all the actors walk straight before them like veritable automata, without taking any notice of the great ideas of the sociologists; they are subject to very simple forces, and not one of them dreams of escaping from the circumstances of his condition. Then only is the development of capitalism carried on with that inevitableness which struck Marx so much, and which seemed to him comparable to that of a natural law. If, on the contrary, the middle class, led astray by the *chatter* of the preachers of ethics and sociology, return to an *ideal of conservative mediocrity*, seek to correct the *abuses* of economics, and wish to break with the barbarism of their predecessors, then one part of the forces which were to further the development of capitalism is employed in hindering it, an arbitrary and irrational element is introduced, and the future of the world becomes completely indeterminate.

This indetermination grows still greater if the proletariat are converted to the ideas of social peace at the same time as their masters, or even if they simply consider everything from the corporative point of view; while Socialism gives to every economic contest a general and revolutionary colour.

Conservatives are not deceived when they see in the compromises which lead to collective contracts, and in corporative particularism, the means of avoiding the Marxian revolution; but they escape one danger only to fall into another, and they run the risk of being devoured by Parliamentary Socialism.

... It is often urged, in objection to the people who defend the Marxian conception, that it is impossible for them to stop the movement of degeneration which is dragging both the middle class and the proletariat far from the paths assigned to them by Marx's theory. They can doubtless influence the working classes, and it is hardly to be denied that strike violences do keep the revolutionary spirit alive; but how can they hope to give back to the middle class an ardour which is spent?

It is here that the role of violence in history appears to us as singularly great, for it can, in an indirect manner, so operate on the middle class as to awaken them to a sense of their own class sentiment. Attention has often been drawn to the danger of certain acts of violence which compromised *admirable social works,* disgusted employers who were disposed to arrange the happiness of their workmen, and developed egoism where the most noble sentiments formerly reigned.

To repay with *black ingratitude* the *benevolence* of those who would protect the workers, to meet with insults the homilies of the defenders of human fraternity, and to reply by blows to the advances of the propagators of social peace—all that is assuredly not in conformity with the rules of the fashionable Socialism . . . but it is a very practical way of indicating to the middle class that they must mind their own business and only that.

I believe also that it may be useful to thrash the orators of democracy and the representatives of the Government, for in this way you insure that none shall retain any illusions about the character of acts of violence. But these acts can have historical value only if they are the *clear and brutal expression of the class war:* the middle classes must not be allowed to imagine that, aided by cleverness, social science, or high-flown sentiments, they might find a better welcome at the hands of the proletariat.

The day on which employers perceive that they have nothing to gain by works which promote social peace, or by democracy, they will understand that they have been ill-advised by the people who persuaded them to abandon their trade of creators of productive forces for the noble profession of educators of the proletariat. Then there is some chance that they may get back a part of their energy, and that moderate or conservative economics may appear as absurd to them as they appeared to Marx. In any case, the separation of classes being more clearly accentuated, the proletarian movement will have some chance of developing with greater regularity than to-day.

The two antagonistic classes therefore influence each other in a partly indirect but decisive manner. Capitalism drives the proletariat into revolt, because in daily life the employers use their force in a direction opposed to the desire of their workers; but the future of the proletariat is not entirely dependent on this revolt; the working classes are organised under the influence of other causes, and Socialism, inculcating in them the revolutionary idea, prepares them to suppress the hostile class. Capitalist force is at the base of all this process, and its action is automatic and inevitable. Marx supposed that the middle class had no need to be incited to employ force, but we are to-day faced with a new and very unforeseen fact-a middle class had no need to be incited its own strength. Must we believe that the Marxian conception is dead? By no means, for proletarian violence comes upon the scene just at the moment when the conception of social peace is being held up as a means of moderating disputes; proletarian violence confines employers to their role of producers, and tends to restore the separation of the classes, just when they seemed on the point of intermingling in the democratic marsh.

Proletarian violence not only makes the future revolution certain, but it seems also to be the only means by which the European nations—at present stupefied by humanitarianism—can recover their former energy. This kind of violence compels capitalism to restrict its attentions solely to its material role and tends to restore to it the warlike qualities which it formerly possessed. A growing and solidly organised working class can compel the capitalist class to remain firm in the industrial war; if a united and revolutionary proletariat confronts a rich middle class, eager for conquest, capitalist society will have reached its historical perfection.

Thus proletarian violence has become an essential factor of Marxism. Let us add once more that, if properly conducted, it will suppress the Parliamentary Socialists, who will no longer be able to pose as the leaders of the working classes and the guardians of order.

. . .The dangers which threaten the future of the world may be avoided, if the proletariat hold on with obstinacy to revolutionary ideas, so as to realise as much as possible Marx's conception. Everything may be saved, if the proletariat, by their use of violence, manage to re-establish the division into classes, and so restore to the middle class something of its former energy; that is the great aim towards which the whole thought of men—who are not hypnotised by the event of the day, but who think of the conditions of to-morrow—must be directed. Proletarian violence, carried on as a pure and simple manifestation of the senti- ment of the class war, appears thus as a very fine and very heroic thing; it is at the service of the immemorial interests of civilisation; it is not perhaps the most appropriate method of obtaining immediate material advantages, but it may save the world from barbarism.

We have a very effective reply to those who accuse Syndicalists of being obtuse and ignorant people. We may ask them to consider the economic deca- dence for which they are working. Let us salute the revolutionaries as the Greek saluted the Spartan heroes who defended Thermopylae and helped to preserve the civilisation of the ancient world.

. . .I think that I have said sufficient to enable me to conclude that if by chance our Parliamentary Socialists get possession of the reins of Government, they will prove to be worthy successors of the Inquisition, of the Old Regime, and of Robespierre; political courts will be at work on a large scale, and we even suppose that the *unfortunate* law of 1848, which abolished the death penalty in political matters, will be repealed. Thanks to this *reform*, we might again see the State triumphing by the hand of the executioner.

Proletarian acts of violence have no resemblance to these proscriptions; they are purely and simply acts of war; they have the value of military demonstrations, and serve to mark the separation of classes. Everything in war is carried on without hatred and without the spirit of revenge: in war the vanquished are not killed; non-combatants are not made to bear the consequences of the disappointments which the armies may have experienced on the fields of battle; force is then displayed according to its own nature, without ever professing to borrow anything from the judicial proceedings which society sets up against criminals.

The more Syndicalism develops, by abandoning the old superstitions which come to it from the Old Regime and from the Church—through the men of letters, professors of philosophy, and historians of the Revolution,—the more will social conflicts assume the character of a simple struggle, similar to those of armies on campaign. We cannot censure too severely those who teach the people that they ought to carry out the highly idealistic decrees of a progressive justice. Their efforts will only result in the maintenance of those ideas about the State which provoked the bloody acts of 1793, whilst the idea of a class war, on the contrary, tends to refine the conception of violence.

*. . . The masses who are led* have a very vague and extremely simple idea of the means by which their lot can be improved; demagogues easily get them to believe that the best way is to utilise the power of the State to *pester* the rich. We pass thus from jealousy to vengeance, and it is well known that vengeance is a sentiment of extraordinary power, especially with the weak. The history of the Greek cities and of the Italian republics of the Middle Ages is full of instances of fiscal laws which were very oppressive on the rich, and which contributed not a little towards the ruin of governments . . . If our contemporary social policy were examined closely, it would be seen that it also was steeped in ideas of jealousy and vengeance; many regulations have been framed more with the idea of pestering employers than of improving the situation of the workers. When the clericals are in a minority, they never fail to recommend severe regulations in order to be revenged on free-thinking free-mason employers.

The leaders obtain all sorts of advantages from these methods; they alarm the rich, and exploit them for their own personal profit; they cry louder than anybody against the privileges of fortune, and know how to obtain for themselves all the enjoyments which the latter procures; by making use of the evil instincts and the stupidity of their followers, they realise this curious paradox, that they get the people to applaud the inequality of conditions in the name of democratic equality. It would be impossible to understand the success of demagogues from the time of Athens to contemporary New York, if due account was not taken of the extraordinary power of the idea of vengeance in extinguishing reasonable reflection.

I believe that the only means by which this pernicious influence of the demagogues may be wiped out are those employed by Socialism in propagating the notion of the proletarian general strike; it awakens in the depths of the soul a sentiment of the sublime proportionate to the conditions of a gigantic struggle; it forces the desire to satisfy jealousy by malice into the background; it brings to the fore the pride of free men, and thus protects the worker from the quackery of ambitious leaders, hungering for the fleshpots.

... The study of the political strike leads us to a better understanding of a distinction we must always have in mind when we reflect on contemporary social questions. Sometimes the terms *force* and *violence* are used in speaking of acts of authority, sometimes in speaking of acts of revolt. It is obvious that the two cases give rise to very different consequences. I think it would be better to adopt a terminology which would give rise to no ambiguity, and that the term *violence* should be employed only for acts of revolt; we should say, therefore, that the object of force is to impose a certain social order in which the minority governs, while violence tends to the destruction of that order. The middle class have used force since the beginning of modern times, while the proletariat now reacts against the middle class and against the State by violence. . . .

## Apology for Violence

Men who make revolutionary speeches to the people are bound to set before themselves a high standard of sincerity, because the workers understand their words in their exact and literal sense, and never indulge in any symbolic interpretation. When in 1905 I ventured to write in some detail on proletarian violence I understood perfectly the grave responsibility I assumed in trying to show the historic bearing of actions which our Parliamentary Socialists try to dissimulate, with so much skill. To-day I do not hesitate to assert that Socialism could not continue to exist without an apology for violence.

It is in strikes that the proletariat asserts its existence. I cannot agree with the view which sees in strikes merely something analogous to the temporary rupture of commercial relations which is brought about when a grocer and the wholesale dealer from whom he buys his dried plums cannot agree about the price. The strike is a phenomenon of war. It is thus a serious misrepresentation to say that violence is an accident doomed to disappear from the strikes of the future.

The social revolution is an extension of that war in which each great strike is an episode; this is the reason why Syndicalists speak of that revolution in the language of strikes; for them Socialism is reduced to the conception, the expectation of, and the preparation for the general strike, which, like the Napoleonic battle, is to completely annihilate a condemned *regime*.

Such a conception allows none of those subtle exegeses in which Jaures excels. It is a question here of an overthrow in the course of which both employers and the State would be set aside by the organised producers. Our Intellectuals, who hope to obtain the highest places from democracy, would be sent back to their literature; the Parliamentary Socialists, who find in the organisations created by the middle classes means of exercising a certain amount of power, would become useless.

The analogy which exists between strikes accompanied by violence and war is prolific of consequences. No one doubts ... that it was war that provided the republics of antiquity with the ideas which form the ornament of our modern culture. The social war, for which the proletariat ceaselessly prepares itself in the syndicates, may engender the elements of a new civilisation suited to a people of producers. I continually call the attention of my young friends to the problems presented by Socialism considered from the point of view of a civilisation of producers; I assert that to-day a philosophy is being elaborated according to this plan, whose possibility even was hardly suspected a few years ago; this philosophy is closely bound up with the apology for violence.

I have never had that admiration for *creative hatred* which Juarès has devoted to it; I do not feel the same indulgence towards the guillotiners as he does; I have a horror of any measure which strikes the vanquished under a judicial disguise. War, carried on in broad daylight, without hypocritical attenuation, for the purpose of ruining an irreconcilable enemy, excludes all the abominations which dishonoured the middle-class revolution of the eighteenth century. The apology for violence in this case is particularly easy.

It would serve no purpose to explain to the poor that they ought not to feel sentiments of jealousy and vengeance against their masters; these feelings are too powerful to be suppressed by exhortations; it is on the widespread prevalence of these feelings that democracy chiefly founds its strength. Social war, by making an appeal to the honour which develops so naturally in all organised armies, can eliminate those evil feelings against which morality would remain powerless. If this were the only reason we had for attributing a high civilising value to revolutionary Syndicalism, this reason alone would, it seems to me, be decisive in favour of the apologists for violence.

The conception of the general strike, engendered by the practice of violent strikes, admits the conception of an irrevocable overthrow. There is something terrifying in this which will appear more and more terrifying as violence takes a greater place in the mind of the proletariat. But, in undertaking a serious, formidable, and sublime work, Socialists raise themselves above our frivolous society and make themselves worthy of pointing out new roads to the world.

Parliamentary Socialists may be compared to the officials whom Napoleon made into a nobility and who laboured to strengthen the State bequeathed by the Ancien Regime. Revolutionary Syndicalism corresponds well enough to the Napoleonic armies whose soldiers accomplished such heroic acts, knowing all the time that they would remain poor. What remains of the Empire? Nothing but the epic of the Grande Armée. What will remain of the present Socialist movement will be the epic of the strikes.

# emmeline pankhurst

Women's liberation movements have assumed a variety of forms in modern history. Political, economic, social, and sexual equality have numbered among the demands made by advocates of female rights. One of the earliest feminist campaigns centered on the fight for political suffrage, and Mrs. Emmeline Pankhurst was one of the ablest and most courageous supporters of that cause. In many ways her task in England was more formidable than that of Susan B. Anthony in America, whose own distinctive achievements were well known to Mrs. Pankhurst because of the comparatively less emancipated status of women in the life and society of Victorian Britain.

Emmeline Pankhurst was born in Manchester, England, on July 14, 1858, the daughter of Robert Goulden, a prosperous calico painter. She received an excellent education and later attended finishing school in Paris, where she befriended the daughter of Henri Rochefort, the French radical. Emmeline married Richard Marsden Pankhurst, a barrister who, as a friend of John Stuart Mill, had drafted the first women's suffrage bill and the subsequent Married Women's Property Acts of 1870 and 1882. The Pankhursts had three daughters, including Christabel (1880-1958) and Sylvia (1882-1960), who were also prominent suffragettes, and two sons. Richard Pankhurst's death in 1898 left Emmeline as the bread-winner of the family, and she took employment as registrar of births and deaths for the city of Manchester.

Emmeline's abiding interest, however, was in the political emancipation of women. Disappointed by the apparent indifference of the Liberal Party, the Fabian Society, and the Independent Labour Party to this cause, she founded the Women's Social and Political Union (W.S.P.U.) in 1903 on nonparty lines. The movement first attracted public attention in 1905, when her daughter Christabel and a friend, Annie Kenny, were thrown out of a British Liberal Party meeting for demanding an answer from Sir Edward Grey about votes for women. Arrested on the charge of technical assault against the police, both girls refused to pay fines ordered by the court and were sent to prison.

In 1906 Mrs. Pankhurst moved to London, where she became increasingly involved in W.S.P.U. activities. With the support of her daughters, together with that of an increasing number of feminists, the W.S.P.U. grew rapidly in numbers, financial resources, and political significance. In 1910, the Liberal Government's sponsorship of suffrage legislation in the form of a "conciliation" bill prompted Mrs. Pankhurst to declare a truce, whereupon her followers obediently suspended their militant programs. But it soon became apparent that British Prime Minister Herbert Asquith's intention was merely to silence rather than to satisfy the suffragettes, particularly after he postponed action on the conciliation bill by virtue of his referral of it to the Committee of the whole House, where proposed legislation usually languished indefinitely.

Mrs. Pankhurst reacted angrily to the treachery of the Liberal Government. On November 18, 1910, the suffragettes conducted a march upon Parliament. In a confrontation with police in Parliament Square, remembered in suffragette history as "Black Friday," a virtual riot ensued for a period of six hours during which hundreds of women were repulsed by police, at first firmly and then violently, as suffragettes attempted to storm the Houses of Parliament. One hundred and fifteen women were arrested before the rioting was finally quelled. The attempt to physically occupy Parliament had failed, but the Government had been profoundly shaken by the horrible brutality which resulted from the suppression of the female militants.

Suffragettes became increasingly more violent, and in 1912 their tactics included the defacing or destruction of public and private buildings and similar targets. Attempts were also made to burn postal boxes, and the Government responded by ordering the arrest of W.S.P.U. leaders on the charge of conspiracy. Christabel received sufficient warning to permit her escape to Paris, where she continued to aid and direct militant suffragettes in London. Mrs. Pankhurst was arrested and sentenced to nine months in prison, but was released within three months following a hunger strike. In June 1913 she was arrested again and sentenced to three years' imprisonment. Her statement before the court on this occasion was an eloquent and forceful declaration of the suffragette position. In it she condemned the Prisoner's (Temporary Discharge for Ill Health) Act of 1913, known as the "Cat and Mouse"Act, whereby hunger-striking prisoners could be temporarily released and re-arrested. She also gave a reasoned argument for the justification of violence and civil disobedience when a political system provides no other alternatives for procuring fundamental human rights. Her testimony in the selection which follows contains lessons and principles which remain timely and are applicable in any number of circumstances in today's society.

Emmeline Pankhurst and her daughter Christabel called off the suffrage campaign at the outbreak of World War I, and the Government released all suffragette prisoners. Many of the same women who had displayed such zeal in seeking to destroy every symbol of British authority responded with equal fervor to the nationalist war effort; some worked in munitions factories while others served as nurses in the fields of Flanders or on the blood-stained beaches of Gallipoli. But Sylvia Pankhurst, the younger of Mrs. Pankhurst's suffragette daughters, continued to demand the vote and broke with her mother and sister by declaring that women should stand for peace, not bloodshed. In February, 1918, the Representation of the People Act gave the vote to a limited number of women. From 1919 to 1925 Mrs. Pankhurst lived in Canada and the United States. Upon her return to England she was selected as a prospective Conservative candidate for an East London constituency in 1926, but the strain of an active lifetime had sapped her vitality, and she died in London on June 14, 1928, a month before the passing of Stanley Baldwin's Representation of the People Act, which gave women full equality in the franchise.

## The Struggle for Women's Suffrage

To account for the phenomenal growth of the Women's Social and Political Union after it was established in London, to explain why it made such an instant appeal to women hitherto indifferent, I shall have to point out exactly wherein our society differs from all other suffrage associations. In the first place, our members are absolutely single minded; they concentrate all their forces on one object, political equality with men. No member of the W.S.P.U. divides her attention between suffrage and other social reforms. We hold that both reason and justice dictate that women shall have a share in reforming the evils that

From Emmeline Pankhurst, *My Own Story*, Hearst's International Library Co., New York, 1914, pp. 57-62, 279-284, 292-299.

afflict society, especially those evils bearing directly on women themselves. Therefore, we demand, before any other legislation whatever, the elementary justice of votes for women.

There is not the slightest doubt that the women of Great Britain would have been enfranchised years ago had all the suffragists adopted this simple principle. They never did, and even to-day many English women refuse to adopt it. They are party members first and suffragists afterward; or they are suffragists part of the time and social theorists the rest of the time. We further differ from other suffrage associations, or from others existing in 1906, in that we clearly perceived the political situation that solidly interposed between us and our enfranchisement.

For seven years we had had a majority in the House of Commons pledged to vote favourably on a suffrage bill. The year before, they had voted favourably on one, yet that bill did not become law. Why? Because even an overwhelming majority of private members are powerless to enact law in the face of a hostile Government of eleven cabinet ministers. The private member of Parliament was once possessed of individual power and responsibility, but Parliamentary usage and a changed conception of statesmanship have gradually lessened the functions of members. At the present time their powers, for all practical purposes, are limited to helping to enact such measures as the Government introduces or, in rare instances, private measures approved by the Government. It is true that the House can revolt, can, by voting a lack of confidence in the Government, force them to resign. But that almost never happens, and it is less likely now than formerly to happen. Figureheads don't revolt.

This, then, was our situation: the Government all-powerful and consistently hostile; the rank and file of legislators impotent; the country apathetic; the women divided in their interests. The Women's Social and Political Union was established to meet this situation and to overcome it. Moreover we had a policy which, if persisted in long enough, could not possibly fail to overcome it. Do you wonder that we gained new members at every meeting we held?

There was little formality about joining the Union. Any woman could become a member by paying a shilling, but at the same time she was required to sign a declaration of loyal adherence to our policy and a pledge not to work for any political party until the women's vote was won. This is still our inflexible custom. Moreover, if at any time a member, or a group of members, loses faith in our policy; if any one begins to suggest that some other policy ought to be substituted, or if she tries to confuse the issue by adding other policies, she ceases at once to be a member. Autocratic? Quite so. But, you may object, a suffrage organisation ought to be democratic. Well the members of the W.S.P.U. do not agree with you. We do not believe in the effectiveness of the ordinary suffrage organisation. The W.S.P.U. is not hampered by a complexity of rules. We have no constitution and by-laws; nothing to be amended or tinkered with or quarrelled over at an annual meeting. In fact, we have no annual meeting, no business sessions, no elections of officers. The W.S.P.U. is simply a suffrage army in the field. It is purely a volunteer army, and no one is obliged to remain in it. Indeed we don't want anybody to remain in it who does not ardently believe in the policy of the army.

The foundation of our policy is opposition to a Government who refuse votes to women. To support by word or deed a Government hostile to woman suffrage is simply to invite them to go on being hostile. We oppose the Liberal party because it is in power. We would oppose a Unionist government if it were in power and were opposed to woman suffrage. We say to women that as long as they remain in the ranks of the Liberal party they give their tacit approval to the Government's anti-suffrage policy. We say to members of Parliament that as long as they support any of the Government's policies they give their tacit approval to the anti-suffrage policy. We call upon all sincere suffragists to leave the Liberal party until women are given votes on equal terms with men. We call upon all voters to vote against Liberal candidates until the Liberal Government does justice to women.

. . . The contention of the old-fashioned suffragists, and of the politicians as well, has always been that an educated public opinion will ultimately give votes to women without any great force being exerted in behalf of the reform. We agree that public opinion must be educated, but we contend that even an educated public opinion is useless unless it is vigorously utilised. The keenest weapon is powerless unless it is courageously wielded. In the year 1906 there was an immensely large public opinion in favour of woman suffrage. But what good did that do the cause? We called upon the public for a great deal more than sympathy. We called upon it to demand of the Government to yield to public opinion and give women votes. And we declared that we would wage war, not only on all anti-suffrage forces, but on all neutral and non-active forces. Every man with a vote was considered a foe to woman suffrage unless he was prepared to be actively a friend.

Not that we believed that the campaign of education ought to be given up. On the contrary, we knew that education must go on, and in much more vigorous fashion than ever before. The first thing we did was to enter upon a sensational campaign to arouse the public to the importance of woman suffrage, and to interest it in our plans for forcing the Government's hands. I think we can claim that our success in this regard was instant, and that it has proved permanent. From the very first, in those early London days, when we were few in numbers and very poor in purse, we made the public aware of the woman suffrage movement as it had never been before. We adopted Salvation Army methods and went out into the highways and the byways after converts. We threw away all our conventional notions of what was "ladylike" and "good form," and we applied to our methods the one test question, Will it help? Just as the Booths and their followers took religion to the street crowds in such fashion that the church people were horrified, so we took suffrage to the general public in a manner that amazed and scandalised the other suffragists.

. . . It was at this time, February, 1913, less that two years ago as I write these words, that militancy, as it is now generally understood by the public began— militancy in the sense of continued, destructive, guerilla warfare against the Government through injury to private property. Some property had been destroyed before this time, but the attacks were sporadic, and were meant to be in the nature of a warning as to what might become a settled policy. Now we indeed lighted the torch, and we did it with the absolute conviction that no other course was open to us. We had tried every other measure, as I am sure that I have demonstrated to my readers, and our years of work and suffering and sacrifice had taught us that the Government would not yield to right and justice, what the majority of members of the House of Commons admitted was right and justice, but that the Government would, as other governments invariably do, yield to expediency. Now our task was to show the Government that it was expedient to yield to the women's just demands. In order to do that we had to make England and every department of English life insecure and unsafe. We had to make English law a failure and the courts farce comedy theatres; we had to discredit the Government and Parliament in the eyes of the world; we had to spoil English sports, hurt business, destroy valuable property, demoralise the world of society, shame the churches, upset the whole orderly conduct of life—

That is, we had to do as much of this guerilla warfare as the people of England would tolerate. When they came to the point of saying to the Government: "Stop this, in the only way it can be stopped, by giving the women of England representation," then we should extinguish our torch.

Americans of all people, ought to see the logic of our reasoning. There is one piece of American oratory, beloved of schoolboys, which has often been quoted from militant platforms. In a speech now included among the classics of the English language your great statesman, Patrick Henry, summed up the causes that led to the American Revolution. He said: "We have petitioned, we have remonstrated, we have supplicated, we have prostrated ourselves at the foot of the throne, and it has all been in vain. We must fight—I repeat it, sir, we must fight."

Patrick Henry, remember, was advocating killing people, as well as destroying private property, as the proper means of securing the political freedom of men. The Suffragettes have not done that, and they never will. In fact the moving spirit of militancy is deep and abiding reverence for human life. In the latter course of our agitation I have been called upon to discuss our policies with many eminent men, politicians, literary men, barristers, scientists, clergymen. One of the last named, a high dignitary of the Church of England, told me that while he was a convinced suffragist, he found it impossible to justify our doing wrong that right might follow. I said to him: "We are not doing wrong—we are doing right in our use of revolutionary methods against private property. It is our work to restore thereby true values, to emphasise the value of human rights against property rights. You are well aware, sir, that property has assumed a value in the eyes of men, and in the eyes of the law, that it ought never to claim. It is placed above all human values. The lives and health and happiness, and even the virtue of women and children—that is to say, the race itself—are being ruthlessly sacrificed to the god of property every day of the world."

To this my reverend friend agreed, and I said: "If we women are wrong in destroying private property in order that human values may be restored, then I say, in all reverence, that it was wrong for the Founder of Christianity to destroy private property, as He did when He lashed the money changers out of the Temple and when He drove the Gaderene swine into the sea."

It was absolutely in this spirit that our women went forth to war. In the first month of guerilla warfare an enormous amount of property was damaged and destroyed. On January 31st a number of putting greens were burned with acids; on February 7th and 8th telegraph and telephone wires were cut in several places and for some hours all communications between London and Glasgow were suspended; a few days later windows in various of London's smartest clubs were broken, and the orchid houses at Kew were wrecked and many valuable blooms destroyed by cold. The jewel room at the Tower of London was invaded and a showcase broken. The residence of H.R.H. Prince Christian and Lambeth Palace, seat of the Archbishop of Canterbury, were visited and had windows broken. The refreshment house in Regents Park was burned to the ground on February 12th and on February 18th a country house which was being built at Walton-on-the-Hill for Mr. Lloyd-George was partially destroyed, a bomb having been exploded in the early morning before the arrival of the workmen. A hat pin and a hair pin picked up near the house—coupled with the fact that care had been taken not to endanger any lives—led the police to believe that the deed had been done by women enemies of Mr. Lloyd-George. Four days later I was arrested and brought up in Epsom police court, where I was charged with having "counselled and procured" the persons who did the damage. Admitted to bail for the night, I appeared next morning in court, where the case was fully reviewed.

... I heard that the authorities had arranged that my trial should take place on April 1st, instead of at the end of June, and at the Central Criminal Court, London, instead of the Guildford Court. I then gave the required undertaking and was immediately released on bail.

... After a hard fight to be allowed to tell the jury the reasons why women had lost respect for the law, and were making such a struggle in order to become law makers themselves, I closed my speech by saying:

"Over one thousand women have gone to prison in the course of this agitation, have suffered their imprisonment, have come out of prison injured in health, weakened in body, but not in spirit. I come to stand my trial from the bedside of one of my daughters, who has come out of Holloway Prison, sent there for two months' hard labour for participating with four other people in breaking a small pane of glass. She has hunger-struck in prison. She submitted herself for more than five weeks to the horrible ordeal of feeding by force, and she has come out of prison having lost nearly two stone in weight. She is so weak that she cannot get out of her bed. And I say to you, gentlemen, that is the kind of punishment you are inflicting upon me or any other woman who may be brought before you. I ask you if you are prepared to send an incalculable number of women to prison—I speak to you as representing others in the same position—if you are prepared to go on doing that kind of thing indefinitely, because that is what is going to happen. There is absolutely no doubt about it. I think you have seen enough even in this present case to convince you that we are not women who are notoriety hunters. We could get that, heaven knows, much more cheaply if we sought it. We are women, rightly or wrongly, convinced that this is the only way in which we can win power to alter what for us are intolerable conditions, absolutely intolerable conditions. A London clergyman only the other day said that 60 per cent of the married women in his parish were breadwinners, supporting their husbands as well as their children. When you think of the wages women earn, when you think of what this means to the future of the children of this country, I ask you to take this question very, very seriously. Only this morning I have had information brought to me which could be supported by sworn affidavits, that there is in this country, in this very city of London of ours, a regulated traffic, not only in women of full age, but in little children; that they are being purchased, that they are being entrapped, and that they are being trained to minister to the vicious pleasures of persons who ought to know better in their positions of life.

"Well, these are the things that have made us women determined to go on, determined to face everything, determined to see this thing out to the end, let it cost us what it may. And if you convict me, gentlemen, if you find me guilty, I tell you quite honestly and quite frankly, that whether the sentence is a long sentence, whether the sentence is a short sentence, I shall not submit to it. I shall, the moment I leave this court, if I am sent to prison, whether to penal servitude or to the lighter form of imprisonment—because I am not sufficiently versed in the law to know what his lordship may decide; but whatever my sentence is, from the moment I leave this court I shall quite deliberately refuse to eat food—I shall join the women who are already in Holloway on the hunger strike. I shall come out of prison, dead or alive, at the earliest possible moment; and once out again, as soon as I am physically fit I shall enter into this fight again. Life is very dear to all of us. I am not seeking, as was said by the Home Secretary, to commit suicide. I do not want to commit suicide. I want to see the women of this country enfranchised, and I want to live until that is done. Those are the feelings by which we are animated. We offer ourselves as sacrifices, just as your forefathers did in the past, in this cause, and I would ask you all to put this question to yourselves:—Have you the right, as human beings, to condemn another human being to death—because that is what it amounts to? Can you throw the first stone? Have you the right to judge women?

"You have not the right in human justice, not the right by the constitution of this country, if rightly interpreted, to judge me, because you are not my peers. You know, every one of you, that I should not be standing here, that I should not break one single law—if I had the rights that you possess, if I had a share in electing those who make the laws I have to obey; if I had a voice in controlling the taxes I am called upon to pay, I should not be standing here. And I say to you it is a very serious state of things. I say to you, my lord, it is a very serious situation, that women of upright life, women who have devoted the best of their years to the public weal, that women who are engaged in trying to undo some of the terrible mistakes that men in their government of the country have made, because after all, in the last resort, men are responsible for the present state of affairs—I put it to you that it is a very serious situation. You are not accustomed to deal with people like me in the ordinary discharge of your duties; but you are called upon to deal with people who break the law from selfish motives. I break the law from no selfish motive. I have no personal end to serve, neither have any of the other women who have gone through this court during the past few weeks, like sheep to the slaughter. Not one of these women would, if women were free, be law-breakers. They are women who seriously believe that this hard path that they are treading is the only path to their enfranchisement. They seriously believe that the welfare of humanity demands this sacrifice; they believe that the horrible evils which are ravaging our civilisation will never be removed until women get the vote. They know that the very fount of life is being poisoned; they know that homes are being destroyed; that because of bad education, because of the unequal standard of morals, even the mothers and children are destroyed by one of the vilest and most horrible diseases that ravage humanity.

"There is only one way to put a stop to this agitation; there is only one way to break down this agitation. It is not by deporting us, it is not by locking us up in gaol; it is by doing us justice. And so I appeal to you gentlemen, in this case of mine, to give a verdict, not only on my case, but upon the whole of this agitation. I ask you to find me not guilty of malicious incitement to a breach of the law.

"These are my last words. My incitement is not malicious. If I had power to deal with these things, I would be in absolute obedience to the law. I would say to women, 'You have a constitutional means of getting redress for your grievances; use your votes, convince your fellow-voters of the righteousness of your demands. That is the way to obtain justice.' I am not guilty of malicious incitement, and I appeal to you, for the welfare of the country, for the welfare of the race, to return a verdict of not guilty in this case that you are called upon to try."

. . . I spoke once more to the Judge.

"The jury have found me guilty, with a strong recommendation to mercy, and I do not see, since motive is not taken into account in human laws, that they could do otherwise after your summing up. But since motive is not taken into account in human laws, and since I, whose motives are not ordinary motives, am about to be sentenced by you to the punishment which is accorded to people whose motives are selfish motives, I have only this to say: If it was impossible for a different verdict to be found; if it is your duty to sentence me, as it will be presently, then I want to say to you, as a private citizen, and to the jury as private citizens, that I, standing here, found guilty by the laws of my country, I say to you it is your duty, as private citizens, to do what you can to put an end to this intolerable state of affairs. I put that duty upon you. And I want to say, *whatever the sentence you pass upon me, I shall do what is humanly possible to terminate that sentence at the earliest possible moment. I have no sense of guilt. I feel I have done my duty. I look upon myself as a prisoner of war. I am under no moral obligation to conform to, or in any way accept, the sentence imposed upon me.* I shall take the desperate remedy that other women have taken. It is obvious to you that the struggle will be an unequal one, but I shall make it—I shall make it as long as I have an ounce of strength left in me, or any life left in me.

"I shall fight, I shall fight, I shall fight, from the moment I enter prison to struggle against overwhelming odds; I shall resist the doctors if they attempt to feed me. I was sentenced last May in this court to nine months' imprisonment. I remained in prison six weeks. There are people who have laughed at the ordeal of hunger-striking and forcible feeding. All I can say is, and the doctors can bear me out, that I was released because, had I remained there much longer, I should have been a dead woman.

"I know what it is because I have gone through it. My own daughter has only just left it. There are women there still facing that ordeal, facing it twice a day. Think of it, my lord, twice a day this fight is gone through. Twice a day a weak woman resisting overwhelming force, fights and fights as long as she has strength left; fights against women and even against men, resisting with her tongue, with her teeth, this ordeal. Last night in the House of Commons some alternative was discussed, or rather, some additional punishment. Is it not a strange thing, my lord, that laws which have sufficed to restrain men throughout the history of this country do not suffice now to restrain women—decent women, honourable women?

"Well, my lord, I do want you to realise it. I am not whining about my punishment. I invited it. I deliberately broke the law, not hysterically or emotionally, but of set serious purpose, because I honestly feel it is the only way. Now, I put the responsibility of what is to follow upon you, my lord, as a private citizen, and upon the gentlemen of the jury, as private citizens, and upon all the men in this court—what are you, with your political powers, going to do to end this intolerable situation?

*"To the women I have represented, to the women who, in response to my incitement, have faced these terrible consequences, have broken laws, to them I want to say I am not going to fail them, but to face it as they face it, to go through with it, and I know that they will go on with the fight whether I live or whether I die.*

*"This movement will go on and on until we have the rights of citizens in this country, as women have in our Colonies, as they will have throughout the civilised world before this woman's war is ended.*

"That is all I have to say."

# lenin

Vladimir Ilyich Ulyanov, who assumed the pseudonym Lenin in 1901, was the greatest single driving force behind the Soviet revolution of November 1917. Born on April 22, 1870, at Simbirsk (later re-named Ulyanov) on the Volga, he was the son of a schoolmaster and the grandson of a physician. Lenin's elder brother, while a university student, was arrested and executed in 1887 for his part in a plot to assassinate Czar Alexander III. This is believed to have turned young Lenin's mind toward revolution; what is certain is that his interests turned toward Marxism and agitation. Expelled from Kazan University for participation in a student demonstration in 1887, he received a degree in law from St. Petersburg University four years later.

By 1895, Lenin was an authority on Marxism, and he travelled abroad during the summer of that year to learn first-hand about European socialism. Upon his return to St. Petersburg he was arrested for his political activities; after spending fourteen months in prison, Lenin was exiled to Siberia for three years in 1897. There he was joined by Nadezhda Krupskaya, whom he had first met at revolutionary functions in St. Petersburg. They were married in July 1898. It was during his exile that Lenin wrote *The Development of Capitalism in Russia,* published in 1899.

Having completed his political exile in 1900, Lenin settled for a time in Pskov (a town near St. Petersburg; the capital was still off-limits to him). There he addressed himself to a dual task: combating the growing influence of revisionist Marxists, like Eduard Bernstein and others in Germany, and building up a strong, strictly centralized party capable of taking complete control of the Marxist movement. In July of 1900 Lenin left Russia for five years, going first to Switzerland, then to Germany, London, Paris, and back to Switzerland. An important document of this period is Lenin's pamphlet *What Is to Be Done?*, composed in the winter of 1901-02, in which he warned that socialism was not natural to the worker and that a vigilant effort would be necessary to cultivate support for the Marxist cause. Another pamphlet, written in March and published in May 1903, which Lenin entitled *To the Rural Poor,* was intended as an explanation for the peasants of what the Social Democrats (Lenin's group) were seeking. It contains a section on political liberty, part of which is reproduced here among the edited selections of Lenin's writings, and provides an excellent illustration of the manner in which the intellectual of the proletariat sought to convert the rural peasant.

Indeed, a landmark in the history of Lenin's political strategy was the new emphasis which, after 1903, he placed upon the possible uses that might be made of the Russian peasantry in the interests of revolution. He came to appreciate how he could enroll the fundamentally conservative peasants on the side of revolution by promising them the property of the landlords. A radical revolution based upon the confiscation of those lands was calculated to appeal more to the peasants than the more limited goals of Russian social democratic reformers who sought the abolition of autocracy in favor of representative government. In another pamphlet published in 1905 and entitled *Two Tactics of Social-Democracy in the Democratic Revolution,* Lenin urged Marxists to remember that in the Social Democrats' war against the bourgeoisie the support of the peasants was essential for any complete victory. Karl Marx had distrusted the land-loving conservative peasants, and this pamphlet, which is included in part among the selections which follow, reveals that Lenin to some degree shared Marx's bias. Lenin bluntly stated that the peasants' allegiance could be won because radical agrarian reform was in their permanent interests. Nowhere did he credit the peasants with anything more than a subordinate role to the proletariat, which he believed to be genuinely committed to the Social Democratic revolution.

Lenin spent a substantial part of his energies after 1907 fighting with fellow socialists whose views on Marx he deemed heretical. Karl Kautsky, the German-Austrian socialist who disputed both Lenin's and Bernstein's revisionist interpretation of Marx, especially irritated Lenin. In addition, he had to combat not only the Mensheviks but also various deviations, philosophical as well as political, within the ranks of his own Bolsheviks.

When the revolution of February-March 1917 broke out in Russia, Lenin was in Switzerland. The German government assisted in his return to St. Petersburg since it knew Lenin to be more intent upon advancing social revolution in Russia than in seeing Germany defeated in World War I. After the Bolshevik-inspired disturbances of July 1917, the provisional Russian government ordered his arrest, but he went into hiding. Lenin continued to write and to guide his party until the provisional government headed by Alexander Kerensky was finally overthrown. Lenin emerged from seclusion on November 7 to become the chairman of the new Soviet government, an office to which he was elected by the revolutionary second congress of soviets. The Bolsheviks asserted that the November Revolution (October according to the old-style Russian calendar) had established a proletarian dictatorship. In fact, Lenin had set up a dictatorship of the Communist party, controlling the hierarchy of all local, regional, and central soviets (committees). Although he could justify dictatorship and the use of terror, as a ruler Lenin could not avoid compromises. He accepted the humiliating peace of Brest-Litovsk (March 1918) from the Germans, and, in the economic sphere, he retreated from orthodox Marxism with his "New Economic Policy." Lenin nevertheless eliminated all organized opposition to his government in a bloody civil war, and also silenced without mercy the hostile factions in his own party.

Russia's revolution of 1917 succeeded in overthrowing the oppressive czarist autocracy, but life in the newly emerged socialist state bore no resemblance to the constitution of the Russian democratic republic which Lenin had called for that same year (see the third selection of the edited entries on Lenin's writings which follow). In May 1922, Lenin suffered a stroke which seriously incapacitated him. On December 16 he had a second stroke and became paralyzed in the right arm and leg. He died on January 21, 1924, at Gorki near Moscow. His legacy is history. Today, more than a third of the world's population live under regimes which consider themselves in the Marxist-Leninist tradition.

## To the Rural Poor

. . . What is political liberty?

To understand this the peasant should first compare his present state of

From *Lenin: Collected Works*, VI, edited by Clemens Dutt and Julius Katzer, Foreign Languages Publishing House, Moscow, 1961, pp. 367-371. This essay was written in April, 1903.

freedom with serfdom. Under the serf-owning system the peasant could not marry without the landlord's permission. Today the peasant is free to marry without anyone's permission. Under the serf-owning system the peasant had unfailingly to work for his landlord on days fixed by the latter's bailiff. Today the peasant is free to decide which employer to work for, on which days, and for what pay. Under the serf-owning system the peasant could not leave his village without the landlord's permission. Today the peasant is free to go wherever he pleases—if the *mir* [landlord] allows him to go, if he is not in arrears with his taxes, if he can get a passport, and if the governor or the police chief does not forbid his changing residence. Thus, even today the peasant is not quite free to go where he pleases; he does not enjoy complete freedom of movement; the peasant is still a semi-serf.

. . . Under the serf-owning system the peasant had no right to acquire property without the landlord's permission; he could not buy land. Today the peasant is free to acquire any kind of property (but even today he is not quite free to leave the *mir*; he is not quite free to dispose of his land as he pleases). Under the serf-owning system the peasant could be flogged by order of the landlord. Today the peasant cannot be flogged by order of the landlord, although he is still liable to corporal punishment.

This freedom is called *civil* liberty—freedom in family matters, in private matters, in matters concerning property. The peasant and the worker are free (although not quite) to arrange their family life and their private affairs, to dispose of their labour (choose their employer) and their property.

But neither the Russian workers nor the Russian people as a whole are yet free to arrange their *public* affairs. The people as a whole are the serfs of the government officials, just as the peasants were the serfs of the landlords. The Russian people have no right to choose their officials, no right to elect representatives to legislate for the whole country. The Russian people have not even the right to arrange meetings for the discussion of *state* affairs. We dare not even print newspapers or books, and dare not even speak to all and for all on matters concerning the whole state without permission from officials who have been put in authority over us without consent, just as the landlord used to appoint his bailiff without the consent of the peasants!

Just as the peasants were the slaves of the landlords, so the Russian people are still the slaves of the officials. Just as the peasants lacked civil freedom under the serf-owning system, so the Russian people still lack *political* liberty. Political liberty means the freedom of the people to arrange their public, state affairs. Political liberty means the right of the people to elect their representatives (deputies) to a State Duma (parliament). All laws should be discussed and passed, all taxes should be fixed only by such a State Duma (parliament) elected

by the people themselves. Political liberty means the right of the people themselves to choose all their officials, arrange all kinds of meetings for the discussion
of all state affairs, and publish whatever papers and books they please, without
having to ask for permission.

All the other European peoples won political liberty for themselves long ago.
Only in Turkey and in Russia are the people still politically enslaved by the
sultan's government and by the tsarist autocratic government. Tsarist autocracy
means the unlimited power of the tsar. The people have no voice in determining
the structure of the state or in running it. All laws are made and all officials are
appointed by the tsar alone, by his personal, unlimited, autocratic authority.
But, of course, the tsar *cannot even know* all Russian laws and all Russian
officials. The tsar cannot even know all that goes on in the country. The tsar
simply endorses the will of a few score of the richest and most high-born officials. However much he may desire to, one man cannot govern a vast country
like Russia. It is not the tsar who governs Russia—it is only a manner of speech
to talk about autocratic, one-man rule! Russia is governed by a handful of the
richest and most high-born officials. The tsar learns only what this handful are
pleased to tell him. The tsar cannot in any way go against the will of this handful
of high-ranking nobles: the tsar himself is a landlord and a member of the
nobility; since his earliest childhood he has lived only among these high-born
people; it was they who brought him up and educated him; he knows about the
Russian people as a whole only that which is known to these noble gentry, these
rich landlords, and the few very rich merchants who are received at the tsar's
Court.

...We must clearly understand what a lie is being told the people by those
who try to make out that tsarist government is the best form of government. In
other countries—those people say—the government is elected; but it is the rich
who are elected, and they govern unjustly and oppress the poor. In Russia the
government is not elected; an autocratic tsar governs the whole country. The tsar
stands above everyone, rich and poor. The tsar, they tell us, is just to everyone,
to the poor and to the rich alike.

Such talk is sheer hypocrisy. Every Russian knows the kind of justice that is
dispensed by our government. Everybody knows whether a plain worker or a
farm labourer in our country can become a member of the State Council. In all
other European countries, however, factory workers and farm-hands have been
elected to the State Duma (parliament); they have been able to speak freely to
all the people about the miserable condition of the workers, and call upon the
workers to unite and fight for a better life. And no one has dared to stop these
speeches of the people's representatives; no policeman has dared to lay a finger
on them.

In Russia there is no elective government, and she is governed not merely by the rich and the high-born, but by the worst of these. She is governed by the most skillful intriguers at the tsar's Court, by the most artful tricksters, by those who carry lies and slanders to the tsar, and flatter and toady to him. They govern in secret; the people do not and cannot know what new laws are being drafted, what wars are being hatched, what new taxes are being introduced, which officials are being rewarded and for what services, and which are being dismissed. In no country is there such a multitude of officials as in Russia. These officials tower above the voiceless people like a dark forest—a mere worker can never make his way through this forest, can never obtain justice. Not a single complaint against bribery, robbery or abuse of power on the part of the officials is ever brought to light; every complaint is smothered in official red tape. The voice of the individual never reaches the whole people, but is lost in this dark jungle, stifled in the police torture chamber. An army of officials, who were never elected by the people and who are not responsible to the people, have woven a thick web, and men and women are struggling in this web like flies.

Tsarist autocracy is an autocracy of officials. Tsarist autocracy means the feudal dependence of the people upon the officials and especially upon the police. Tsarist autocracy is police autocracy.

That is why the workers come out into the streets with banners bearing the inscriptions: "Down with the autocracy!", "Long live political liberty!" That is why the tens of millions of the rural poor must also support and take up this battle-cry of the urban workers. Like them, undaunted by persecution, fearless of the enemy's threats and violence, and undeterred by the first reverses, the agricultural labourers and the poor peasants must come forward for a decisive struggle for the freedom of the whole of the Russian people and demand first of all the *convocation of the representatives of the people*. Let the people themselves all over Russia elect their representatives (deputies). Let those representatives form a supreme assembly, which will introduce elective government in Russia, free the people from feudal dependence upon the officials and the police, and secure for the people the right to meet freely, speak freely, and have a free press!

That is what the Social-Democrats want first and foremost. That is the meaning of their first demand: the *demand for political liberty*.

## Two Tactics of Social Democracy in the Democratic Revolution

... The very position the bourgeoisie holds as a class in capitalist society inevitably leads to its inconsistency in a democratic revolution. The very position the proletariat holds as a class compels it to be consistently democratic. The bourgeoisie looks backward in fear of democratic progress which threatens to strengthen the proletariat. The proletariat has nothing to lose but its chains, but with the aid of democratism it has the whole world to win. That is why the more consistent the bourgeois revolution is in achieving its democratic transformations, the less will it limit itself to what is of advantage exclusively to the bourgeoisie. The more consistent the bourgois revolution, the more does it guarantee the proletariat and the peasantry the benefits accruing from the democratic revolution.

Marxism teaches the proletarian not to keep aloof from the bourgeois revolution, not to be indifferent to it, not to allow the leadership of the revolution to be assumed by the bourgeoisie but, on the contrary, to take a most energetic part in it, to fight most resolutely for consistent proletarian democratism, for the revolution to be carried to its conclusion. We cannot get out of the bourgeois-democratic boundaries of the Russian revolution, but we can vastly extend these boundaries, and within these boundaries we can and must fight for the interests of the proletariat, for its immediate needs and for conditions that will make it possible to prepare its forces for the future complete victory.

... A Social-Democrat must never for a moment forget that the proletariat will inevitably have to wage a class struggle for socialism even against the most democratic and republican bourgeoisie and petty bourgeoisie. This is beyond doubt. Hence, the absolute necessity of a separate, independent, strictly class party of Social-Democracy. Hence, the temporary nature of our tactics of "striking a joint blow" with the bourgeoisie and the duty of keeping a strict watch "over our ally, as over an enemy," etc. All this also leaves no room for doubt. However, it would be ridiculous and reactionary to deduce from this that we must forget, ignore, or neglect tasks which, although transient and temporary, are vital at the present time. The struggle against the autocracy is a temporary and transient task for socialists, but to ignore or neglect this task in any way amounts to betrayal of socialism and service to reaction. The revolutionary-democratic dictatorship of the proletariat and the peasantry is unques-

From *Lenin: Collected Works,* IX, edited by George Hanna, Foreign Languages Publishing House, Moscow, 1962, pp. 51-52, 85-86, 97-100, 108-109, 113. This essay was written in July 1905.

tionably only a transient, temporary socialist aim, but to ignore this aim in the period of a democratic revolution would be downright reactionary.

... Have you, gentlemen, ever given thought to real social forces that determine "the sweep of the revolution"? Let us disregard the foreign political forces, the international combinations, which have developed very favourably for us at the present time, but which we all leave out of the discussion, and rightly so, inasmuch as we are concerned with the question of Russia's internal forces. Examine these internal social forces. Aligned against the revolution are the autocracy, the imperial court, the police, the bureaucracy, the army, and a handful of the aristocracy. The deeper the indignation of the people grows, the less reliable the troops become, and the more the bureaucracy wavers. Moreover, the bourgeoisie, on the whole, is now in favour of revolution, zealously speechifying about liberty and holding forth more and more frequently in the name of the people and even in the name of the revolution. But we Marxists all know from theory and from daily and hourly observation of our liberals, Zemstvo people, and *Osvobozhdeniye* supporters, that the bourgeoisie is inconsistent, self-seeking, and cowardly in its support of the revolution. The bourgeoisie, in the mass, will inevitably turn towards counter-revolution, towards the autocracy, against the revolution, and against the people, as soon as its narrow, selfish interests are met, as soon as it "recoils" from consistent democracy (*and it is already recoiling from it*)! There remains the "people", that is, the proletariat and the peasantry: the proletariat alone can be relied on to march on to the end, for it goes far beyond the democratic revolution. That is why the proletariat fights in the forefront for a republic and contemptuously rejects stupid and unworthy advice to take into account the possibility of the bourgeoisie recoiling. The peasantry includes a great number of semi-proletarian as well as petty-bourgeois elements. This makes it also unstable, compelling the proletariat to rally in a strictly class party. However, the instability of the peasantry differs radically from that of the bourgeoisie, for at present the peasantry is interested not so much in the absolute preservation of private property as in the confiscation of the landed estates, one of the principal forms of private property. Without thereby becoming socialist, or ceasing to be petty-bourgeois, the peasantry is capable of becoming a wholehearted and most radical adherent of the democratic revolution. The peasantry will inevitably become such if only the course of revolutionary events, which brings it enlightenment, is not prematurely cut short by the treachery of the bourgeoisie and the defeat of the proletariat. Subject to this condition the peasantry will inevitably become a bulwark of the revolution and the republic, for only a completely victorious revolution can give the peasantry *everything* in the sphere of agrarian reforms—*everything* that the peasants desire, dream of, and truly need (not for the abolition of capitalism as the "Socialist-Revolutionaries" imagine, but) in order to emerge from the mire of semi-serfdom, from the gloom of oppression and servitude, in order to improve their living conditions, as much as they can be improved within the system of commodity production.

Moreover, it is not only by the prospect of radical agrarian reform that the peasantry is attached to the revolution, but by all its general and permanent interests as well. Even when fighting with the proletariat, the peasantry stands in need of democracy, for only a democratic system is capable of accurately expressing its interests and ensuring its predominance as a mass, as the majority. The more enlightened the peasantry becomes (and since the war with Japan it is becoming enlightened at a pace unsuspected by many who are accustomed to measure enlightenment with the school yardstick), the more consistently and resolutely will it stand for a thoroughgoing democratic revolution; for, unlike the bourgeoisie, it has nothing to fear from the people's supremacy, but on the contrary stands to gain by it. A democratic republic will become the peasantry's ideal as soon as it begins to throw off its naive monarchism, because the conscious monarchism of the bourgeois stock-jobbers (with an upper chamber, etc.) implies for the peasantry the same absence of rights and the same oppression and ignorance as it suffers today, only slightly polished over with the varnish of European constitutionalism.

That is why, as a class, the bourgeoisie naturally and inevitably tends to come under the wing of the liberal-monarchist party, while the peasantry, in the mass, tends to come under the leadership of the revolutionary and republican party. That is why the bourgeoisie is incapable of carrying through the democratic revolution to its consummation, while the peasantry is capable of doing so, and we must exert all our efforts to help it do so.

... *The proletariat must carry the democratic revolution to completion, allying to itself the mass of the peasantry in order to crush the autocracy's resistance by force and paralyse the bourgeoisie's instability. The proletariat must accomplish the socialist revolution, allying to itself the mass of the semi-proletarian elements of the population, so as to crush the bourgeoisie's resistance by force and paralyse the instability of the peasantry and the petty bourgeoisie.*

... Perhaps the most vivid expression of this rift between the intellectual opportunist wing and the proletarian revolutionary wing of the Party was the question: *durfen wir siegen?* "Dare we win?" Is it permissible for us to win? Would it not be dangerous for us to win? Ought we to win? This question, so strange at first sight, was however raised and had to be raised, because the opportunists were afraid of victory, were frightening the proletariat away from it, predicting that trouble would come of it and ridiculing slogans that straight-forwardly called for it.

The same fundamental division into an intellectual-opportunist and prole-tarian-revolutionary trend exists among us too, with the very material difference, however, that here we are faced with the question of a democratic, not of a socialist revolution. The question "dare we win?" which seems so absurd at first sight, has been raised among us as well. It has been raised by Martynov in his *Two Dictatorships,* wherein he prophesies dire misfortune if we prepare well for an insurrection, and carry it out quite successfully.

. . . And although Kautsky, for instance, now tries to wax ironical and says that our dispute about a provisional revolutionary government is like sharing out the meat before the bear is killed, this irony only proves that even clever and revolutionary Social-Democrats are liable to put their foot in it when they talk about something they know of only by hearsay. German Social-Democracy is not yet so near to killing its bear (carrying out a socialist revolution), but the dispute as to whether we "dare" kill the bear has been of enormous importance from the point of view of principles and of practical politics. Russian Social-Democrats are not yet so close to being able to "kill their bear" (carry out a democratic revolution), but the question as to whether we "dare" kill it is of extreme importance to the whole future of Russia and that of Russian Social-Democracy. An army cannot be energetically and successfully mustered and led unless we are sure that we "dare" win.

. . . Revolutions are the locomotives of history, said Marx. Revolutions are festivals of the oppressed and the exploited. At no other time are the mass of the people in a position to come forward so actively as creators of a new social order, as at a time of revolution. At such times the people are capable of performing miracles, if judged by the limited, philistine yardstick of gradualist progress. But it is essential that leaders of the revolutionary parties, too, should advance their aims more comprehensively and boldly at such a time, so that their slogans shall always be in advance of the revolutionary initiative of the masses, serve as a beacon, reveal to them our democratic and socialist ideal in all its magnitude and splendour, and show them the shortest and most direct route to complete, absolute, and decisive victory.

## Revision of the Party Program

. . . The constitution of the Russian democratic republic must ensure:

1. The sovereignty of the people; supreme power in the state must be vested entirely in the people's representatives, who shall be elected by the people and be subject to recall at any time, and who shall constitute a single popular assembly, a single chamber.

2. Universal, equal, and direct suffrage for all citizens, men and women, who have reached the age of twenty, in the elections to the legislative assembly and to the various bodies of local self-government; secret ballot; the right of every voter to be elected to any representative institution; biennial parliaments; salaries to be paid to the people's representatives; proportional representation to all elections; all delegates and elected officials, without exception, to be subject to recall at any time upon the decision of a majority of their electors.

3. Local self-government on a broad scale; regional self-government in localities where the composition of the population and living and social conditions are of a specific nature; the abolition of all state-appointed local and regional authorities.

4. Inviolability of person and domicile.

5. Unrestricted freedom of conscience, speech, the press, assembly, strikes, and association.

6. Freedom of movement and occupation.

7. Abolition of the social estates; equal rights for all citizens irrespective of sex, creed, race, or nationality.

8. The right of the population to receive instruction in their native tongue in schools to be established for the purpose at the expense of the state and local organs of self-government; the right of every citizen to use his native language at meetings; the native language to be used in all local public and state institutions; the obligatory official language to be abolished.

9. The right of all member nations of the state to freely secede and form independent states. The republic of the Russian nation must attract other nations or nationalities not by force, but exclusively by voluntary agreement on the question of forming a common state. The unity and fraternal alliance of the workers of all countries are incompatible with the use of force, direct or indirect, against other nationalities.

10. The right of all persons to sue any official in the regular way before a jury.

11. Judges and other officials, both civil and military, to be elected by the

From *Lenin: Collected Works*, XXIV, edited by Bernard Isaacs, Progress Publishers, Moscow, 1964, pp. 471-477. This essay was written in May 1917.

people with the right to recall any of them at any time by decision of a majority of their electors.

12. The police and standing army to be replaced by the universally armed people; workers and other employees to receive regular wages from the capitalists for the time devoted to public service in the people's militia.

13. Separation of the church from the state, and schools from the church; schools to be absolutely secular.

14. Free and compulsory general and polytechnical education (familiarising the student with the theoretical and practical aspects of the most important fields of production) for all children of both sexes up to the age of sixteen; training of children to be closely integrated with socially productive work.

15. All students to be provided with food, clothing, and school supplies at the cost of the state.

16. Public education to be administered by democratically elected organs of local self-government; the central government not to be allowed to interfere with the arrangement of the school curriculum, or with the selection of the teaching staffs; teachers to be elected directly by the population with the right of the latter to remove undesirable teachers.

As a basic condition for the democratisation of our country's national economy, the Russian Social-Democratic Labour Party demands the abolition of all indirect taxes and the establishment of a progressive tax on incomes and inheritances.

The high level of development of capitalism already achieved in banking and in the trustified branches of industry, on the one hand, and the economic disruption caused by the imperialist war, everywhere evoking a demand for state and public control of the production and distribution of all staple products, on the other, induce the party to demand the nationalisation of the banks, syndicates (trusts), etc.

To safeguard the working class from physical and moral deterioration, and develop its ability to carry on the struggle for emancipation, the Party demands:

1. An eight-hour working day for all wage-workers, including a break of not less than one hour for meals where work is continuous. In dangerous and unhealthy industries the working day to be reduced to from four to six hours.

2. A statutory weekly uninterrupted rest period of not less than forty-two hours for all wage-workers of both sexes in all branches of the national economy.

3. Complete prohibition of overtime work.

4. Prohibition of night-work (from 8 p.m. to 6 a.m.) in all branches of the national economy except in cases where it is absolutely necessary for technical reasons endorsed by the labour organisations—provided, however, that night-work does not exceed four hours.

5. Prohibition of the employment of children of *school* age (under sixteen), restriction of the working day of adolescents (from sixteen to twenty) to four hours, and prohibition of the employment of adolescents on night-work in unhealthy industries and mines.

6. Prohibition of female labour in all branches of industry injurious to women's health; prohibition of night work for women; women to be released from work eight weeks before and eight weeks after child-birth without loss of pay and with free medical and medicinal aid.

7. Establishment of nurseries for infants and young children and rooms for nursing mothers at all factories and other enterprises where women are employed; nursing mothers to be allowed recesses of at least half-hour duration at intervals of not more than three hours; such mothers to receive nursing benefit and their working day to be reduced to six hours.

8. Full social insurance of workers:

a) for all forms of wage-labour;

b) for all forms of disablement, namely, sickness, injury, infirmity, old age, occupational disease, childbirth, widowhood, orphanhood, and also unemployment, etc.

c) all insurance institutions to be administered entirely by the insured themselves;

d) the cost of insurance to be borne by the capitalists;

e) free medical and medicinal aid under the control of self-governing sick benefit societies, the management bodies of which are to be elected by the workers.

9. The establishment of a labour inspectorate elected by the workers' organisations and covering all enterprises employing hired labour, as well as domestic servants; women inspectors to be appointed in enterprises where female labour is employed.

10. Sanitary laws to be enacted for improving hygienic conditions and protecting the life and health of workers in all enterprises where hired labour is employed; questions of hygiene to be handled by the sanitary inspectorate elected by the workers' organisations.

11. Housing laws to be enacted and a housing inspectorate elected by the workers' organisations to be instituted for the purpose of sanitary inspection of dwelling houses. However, only by abolishing private property in land and building cheap and hygienic dwellings can the housing problem be solved.

12. Industrial courts to be established in all branches of the national economy.

13. Labour exchanges to be established for the proper organisation of work-finding facilities. These labour exchanges must be proletarian class organisations (organised on a non-parity basis), and must be closely associated with the trade

unions and other working-class organisations and financed by the communal self-governing bodies.

## A Great Beginning

... And what does the "abolition of classes" mean? All those who call themselves socialists recognize this as the ultimate goal of socialism, but by no means all give thought to its significance. Classes are large groups of people differing from each other by the place they occupy in a historically determined system of social production, by their relation (in most cases fixed and formulated in law) to the means of production, by their role in the social organisation of labour, and, consequently, by the dimensions of the share of social wealth of which they dispose and the mode of acquiring it. Classes are groups of people one of which can appropriate the labour of another owing to the different places they occupy in a definite system of social economy.

Clearly, in order to abolish classes completely, it is not enough to overthrow the exploiters, the landowners and capitalists, not enough to abolish *their* rights of ownership; it is necessary also to abolish *all* private ownership of the means of production, it is necessary to abolish the distinction between town and country, as well as the distinction between manual workers and brain workers. This requires a very long period of time. In order to achieve this an enormous step forward must be taken in developing the productive forces; it is necessary to overcome the resistance (frequently passive, which is particularly stubborn and particularly difficult to overcome) of the numerous survivals of small-scale production; it is necessary to overcome the enormous force of habit and conservatism which are connected with these survivals.

The assumption that all "working people" are equally capable of doing this work would be an empty phrase, or the illusion of an antediluvian, pre-Marxist socialist; for this ability does not come of itself, but grows historically, and grows *only* out of the material conditions of large-scale capitalist production. This ability, at the beginning of the road from capitalism to socialism, is possessed by the proletariat *alone*.

... Notwithstanding all the laws emancipating woman, she continues to be a *domestic slave,* because *petty housework* crushes, strangles, stultifies and de-

From *Lenin: Collected Works*, XXIX, edited by George Hanna, Progress Publishers, Moscow, 1965, pp. 421, 429-430. This essay was written in July 1919.

grades her, chains her to the kitchen and the nursery, and she wastes her labour on barbarously unproductive, petty, nerve-racking, stultifying and crushing drudgery. The real *emancipation of women,* real communism, will begin only where and when an all-out struggle begins (led by the proletariat wielding the state power) against this petty housekeeping, or rather when its *wholesale transformation* into a large-scale socialist economy begins.

Do we in practice pay sufficient attention to this question, which in theory every Communist considers indisputable? Of course not. Do we take proper care of the *shoots* of communism which already exist in this sphere? Again the answer is *no* Public catering establishments, nurseries, kindergartens—here we have examples of these shoots, here we have the simple, everyday means, involving nothing pompous, grandiloquent or ceremonial, which can *really emancipate women,* really lessen and abolish their inequality with men as regards their role in social production and public life. These means are not new, they (like all the material prerequisites for socialism) were created by large-scale capitalism. But under capitalism they remained, first, a rarity, and secondly—which is particularly important—either *profit-making* enterprises, with all the worst features of speculation, profiteering, cheating and fraud, or "acrobatics of bourgeois charity," which the best workers rightly hated and despised.

There is no doubt that the number of these institutions in our country has increased enormously and that they are *beginning* to change in character. There is no doubt that we have far more *organising talent* among the working and peasant women than we are aware of, that we have far more people than we know of who can organise practical work, with the co-operation of large numbers of workers and of still larger numbers of consumers, without that abundance of talk, fuss, squabbling and chatter about plans, systems, etc., with which our big-headed "intellectuals" or half-baked "Communists" are "affected." But we *do not nurse* these shoots of the new as we should.

# james connolly

James Connolly was a socialist and Irish Republican leader who played a decisive part in the Dublin Easter Uprising of 1916. Born near Clones, County Monaghan, Connolly was the son of a laborer, and from his earliest years he waged a struggle with poverty. When he was ten years old his family was forced, like countless others of their class, to seek work in Scotland. It was there that Connolly received his earliest experience with the socialist movement as a member of the Social Democratic Federation. He later spent seven years, from 1903 to 1910, in the United States, where he helped organize the Industrial Workers of the World. His sincerity and ability as a leader gained him the respect of organized workers. Upon his return from America, Connolly began promoting the socialist cause in Ireland. He championed the rights of the miserably underpaid women workers in Belfast and, in 1911, led demonstrations on behalf of the dock laborers in Dublin and other Irish ports. Connolly became James Larkin's chief assistant in organizing the Irish National Transport Union, which sought to enroll all Irish workers' support in every labor dispute. Reacting to a number of carefully staged "sympathetic strikes," Dublin employers joined to break Larkin's union in 1913 through a ruthless lockout.

It was partly as a response to the brutal dispersion of labor demonstrations by the authorities that Connolly formed the Citizen Army in 1913. Fundamentally a Marxist who was concerned with the exploitation of the working class in an industrial age, Connolly was not unaware of the importance of peasant support to the urban labor movement, or the fact that the peasants made up the vast majority of Ireland's population. Long before his theories were tested by the Russian Revolution of 1917, he was concerned with the "potential conflict" between town and country after the defeat of capitalism. Like Lenin, he realized the possible role of co-operatives in securing unity between the proletariat and the peasant, not only in the economic field, but also eventually in the political field.

Larkin was in the United States at the outbreak of World War I, and Connolly assumed charge of the Irish labor movement and committed it to opposing the Allied war effort; he insisted that peace could come only through the overthrow of all capitalist states. Because of his conviction that the triumph of Irish nationalism was a prerequisite for the success of Irish socialism, he joined the Easter Rebellion of 1916. Connolly's temporary military alliance with the Irish bourgeois nationalists did not prevent him from leveling scornful attacks at their leaders; he never ceased insisting that the ultimate freedom of the Irish people would be achieved only after they had seized control over the means and modes of production in Ireland. The bourgeois nationalist goal of political independence without sweeping social reform held no attraction for him. When the Dublin rising was suppressed after a week of fighting and considerable bloodshed, the wounded Connolly was executed along with other leaders of the insurrection.

With the exception of a few published works, the writings of James Connolly lie buried in museum files of obscure periodicals. His writings and achievements in Ireland have often been suppressed and distorted, and these distortions have served to bewilder that wider world audience which today stands in need of the lessons of his life and leadership. His non-sectarian support included members of both the Protestant and Catholic working class in Ulster. His eloquent condemnation of war, his vision of a free nation, and his concept of the socialist goal appear in the three essays which follow. His philosophy is perhaps best summarized in an excerpt from an editorial published in Connolly's labor newspaper, *The Worker's Republic,* on May 29, 1915:

In the long run the freedom of a nation is measured by the freedom of its lowest class; every upward step of that class to the possibility of possessing higher things raises the standard of the nation in the scale of civilization; every time that class is beaten back into the mire, the whole moral tone of the nation suffers. Condemned and despised though he may be, yet the rebellious docker is the sign and symbol that an imperfect civilization cannot last, for slavery cannot survive the awakened intelligence of the slave.

# A War for Civilization

We are hearing and reading a lot just now about a war for civilization. In some vague, ill-defined manner we are led to believe that the great empires of Europe have suddenly been seized with a chivalrous desire to right the wrongs of mankind, and have sallied forth to war, giving their noblest blood and greatest treasures to the task of furthering the cause of civilization.

... This War for Civilization in the name of neutrality and small nationalities invades Persia and Greece, and in the name of the interests of commerce seizes the cargo of neutral ships, and flaunts its defiance of neutral flags.

In the name of freedom from militarism it establishes military rule in Ireland; battling for progress it abolishes trial by jury; and waging war for enlightened rule it tramples the freedom of the Press under the heel of a military despot.

Is it any wonder, then, that this particular War for Civilization arouses no enthusiasm in the ranks of the toiling masses of the Irish nation?

But there is another war for civilization in which these masses are interested. That war is being waged by the forces of organized Labour.

Civilization cannot be built upon slaves; civilization cannot be secured if the producers are sinking into misery; civilization is lost if they whose labour makes it possible share so little of its fruits that its fall can leave them no worse than its security.

The workers are at the bottom of civilized society. That civilization may endure they ought to push upward from their poverty and misery until they emerge into the full sunlight of freedom. When the fruits of civilization, created by all, are enjoyed in common by all then civilization is secure. Not till then.

Since this European war started, the workers as a whole have been sinking. It is not merely that they have lost in comfort—have lost a certain standard of food and clothing by reason of the increase of prices—but they have lost in a great measure, in England at least, all those hard-won rights of combination, of freedom of action, the possession of which was the foundation upon which they hoped to build the greater freedom of the future.

From being citizens with rights, the workers are being driven and betrayed into the position of slaves with duties. Some of them may have been well-paid slaves, but slavery is not measured by the amount of oats in the feeding trough to which the slave is tied; it is measured by his loss of control of the conditions under which he labours.

We here in Ireland, particularly those who follow the example of the Transport Union, have been battling to preserve those rights which others have sur-

From *The Workers' Republic*, October 30, 1915, pp. 51, 53-55.

rendered. We have fought to keep up our standards of life, to force up our wages, to better our conditions.

To that extent we have truly been engaged in a war for civilization. Every victory we have gained has gone to increase the security of life amongst our class, has gone to put bread on the tables, coals in the fires, clothes on the backs of those to whom food and warmth and clothing are things of ever-pressing moment.

Some of our class have fought in Flanders and the Dardanelles; the greatest achievement of them all combined will weigh but a feather in the balance for good compared with the achievements of those who stayed at home and fought to secure the rights of the working class against invasion.

The carnival of murder on the Continent will be remembered as a nightmare in the future, will not have the slightest effect in deciding for good the fate of our homes, our wages, our hours, our conditions. But the victories of Labour in Ireland will be as footholds, secure and firm, in the upward climb of our class to the fulness and enjoyment of all that Labour creates and organized society can provide.

Truly, Labour alone in these days is fighting the real WAR FOR CIVILI-ZATION.

## What is a Free Nation?

We are moved to ask this question because of the extraordinary confusion of thought upon the subject which prevails in this country, due principally to the pernicious and misleading newspaper garbage upon which the Irish public has been fed for the past twenty-five years.

Our Irish daily newspapers have done all that human agencies could do to confuse the public mind upon the question of what the essentials of a free nation are, what a free nation must be, and what a nation cannot submit to lose without losing its title to be free.

It is because of this extraordinary newspaper-created ignorance that we find so many people enlisting in the British Army under the belief that Ireland has at long last attained to the status of a free nation, and that therefore the relations between Ireland and England have at last been placed upon the satisfactory basis of freedom. Ireland and England, they have been told, are now sister nations,

From *The Workers' Republic*, February 12, 1916, pp. 108, 110-114.

joined in the bond of Empire, but each enjoying equal liberties—the equal liberties of nations equally free.

How many recruits this idea sent into the British Army in the first flush of the war it would be difficult to estimate, but they were assuredly numbered by the thousand.

...Our Parliamentarians treat Ireland, their country, as an old prostitute selling her soul for the promise of favours *to come,* and in the spirit of that conception of their country they are conducting their political campaign.

...What is a free nation? A free nation is one which possesses absolute control over all its own internal resources and powers, and which has no restrictions upon its intercourse with all other nations similarly circumstanced except the restrictions placed upon it by nature. Is that the case of Ireland? If the Home Rule Bill were in operation would that be the case of Ireland? To both questions the answer is, No, most emphatically, NO!

A free nation must have complete control over its own harbours, to open them or close them at will, to shut out any commodity, or allow it to enter in, just as it seems best to suit the well-being of its own people, and in obedience to their wishes, and entirely free of the interference of any other nation, and in complete disregard of the wishes of any other nation. Short of that power no nation possesses the first essentials of freedom.

Does Ireland possess such control? No. Will the Home Rule Bill give such control over Irish harbours to Ireland? It will not. Ireland must open its harbours when it suits the interests of another nation, England, and must shut its harbours when it suits the interests of another nation, England, and the Home Rule Bill pledges Ireland to accept this loss of national control for ever.

How would you like to live in a house if the keys of all the doors of that house were in the pockets of a rival of yours who had often robbed you in the past? Would you be satisfied if he told you that he and you were going to be friends for ever more, but insisted upon you signing an agreement to leave him control of all your doors, and custody of all your keys?

That is the condition of Ireland to-day, and will be the condition of Ireland under Redmond and Devlin's precious Home Rule Bill.

That is worth dying for in Flanders, the Balkans, Egypt or India, is it not?

A free nation must have full power to nurse industries to health, either by Government encouragement, or by Government prohibition of the sale of goods of foreign rivals. It may be foolish to do either, but a nation is not free unless it has that power, as all free nations in the world have to-day.

Ireland has no such power, will have no such power under Home Rule. The nourishing of industries in Ireland hurts capitalists in England, therefore this power is expressly withheld from Ireland.

A free nation must have full power to alter, amend, or abolish or modify the laws under which the property of its citizens is held in obedience to the demand of its own citizens for any such alteration, amendment, abolition, or modification.

Every free nation has that power; Ireland does not have it, and is not allowed it by the Home Rule Bill.

It is recognized to-day that it is upon the wise treatment of economic power and resources, and upon the wise ordering of social activities that the future of nations depends. That nation will be the richest and happiest which has the foresight to most carefully marshal its natural resources to national ends. But Ireland is denied this power, and will be denied it under Home Rule. Ireland's rich natural resources, and the kindly genius of its children, are not to be allowed to combine for the satisfaction of Irish wants, save in so far as their combination can operate on lines approved of by the rulers of England.

Her postal service, her telegraphs, her wireless, her customs and excise, her coinage, her fighting forces, her relations with other nations, her merchant commerce, her property relations, her national activities, her legislative sovereignty— all, all the things that are essential to a nation's freedom are denied to Ireland now, and are denied to her under the provisions of the Home Rule Bill.

And Irish soldiers in the English Army are fighting in Flanders to win for Belgium, we are told, all those things which the British Empire, now as in the past, denies to Ireland.

. . . There is not a pacifist in England who would wish to end the war without Belgium being restored to full possession of all those national rights and powers which Ireland does not possess, and which the Home Rule Bill denies to her. But these same pacifists never mention Ireland when discussing or suggesting terms of settlement.

Why should they? Belgium is fighting for her independence, but Irishmen are fighting for the Empire that denies Ireland every right that Belgians think worth fighting for.

And yet Belgium as a nation is, so to speak, but a creation of yesterday—an artificial product of the schemes of statesmen; whereas the frontiers of Ireland, the ineffaceable marks of the separate existence of Ireland, are as old as Europe itself, the handiwork of the Almighty, not of politicians. And as the marks of Ireland's separate nationality were not made by politicians so they cannot be unmade by them.

. . . There can be no perfect Europe in which Ireland is denied even the least of its national rights; there can be no worthy Ireland whose children brook tamely such denial.

If such denial has been accepted by soulless slaves of politicians, then it must be repudiated by Irish men and women whose souls are still their own.

The peaceful progress of the future requires the possession by Ireland of all the national rights now denied to her. Only in such possession can the workers of Ireland see stability and security for the fruits of their toil and organization.

A destiny not of our fashioning has chosen this generation as the one called upon for the supreme act of self-sacrifice—to die if need be that our race might live in freedom.

Are we worthy of the choice? Only by our response to the call can that question be answered.

## What Is Our Programme?

We are often asked the above question.

...The Labour movement is like no other movement. Its strength lies in being like no other movement. It is never so strong as when it stands alone. Other movements dread analysis and shun all attempts to define their objects. The Labour movement delights in analyzing and is perpetually defining and re-defining its principles and objects.

The man or woman who has caught the spirit of the Labour movement brings that spirit of analysis and definition into all public acts, and expects at all times to answer the call to define his or her position. They cannot live on illusions, nor thrive by them; even should their heads be in the clouds they will make no forward step until they are assured that their feet rest upon the solid earth.

... What is our programme? We at least, in conformity with the spirit of our movement, will try and tell it.

Our programme in time of peace was to gather into Irish hands in Irish Trade Unions the control of all the forces of production and distribution in Ireland. We never believed that freedom would be realized without fighting for it. From our earliest declaration of policy in Dublin in 1896 the editor of this paper has held to the dictum that our ends should be secured "peacefully if possible, forcibly if necessary." Believing so, we saw what the world outside Ireland is realizing to-day, that the destinies of the world and the fighting strength of armies are at the mercy of organized Labour as soon as that Labour becomes truly revolutionary. Thus we strove to make Labour in Ireland organized—and revolutionary.

From *The Workers' Republic*, January 22, 1916, pp. 120-125.

We saw that should it come to a test in Ireland (as we hoped and prayed it might come) between those who stood for the Irish nation and those who stood for the foreign rule, the greatest civil asset in the hand of the Irish nation for use in the struggle would be the control of Irish docks, shipping, railways and production by Unions who gave sole allegiance to Ireland.

We realized that the power of the enemy to hurl his forces upon the forces of Ireland would lie at the mercy of the men who controlled the transport system of Ireland; we saw that the hopes of Ireland as a nation rested upon the due recognition of the identity of interest between that ideal and the rising hopes of Labour.

. . . Have we a programme? We are the only people that had a programme—that understood the mechanical conditions of modern war, and the dependence of national power upon industrial control.

What is our programme now? At the grave risk of displeasing alike the per-fervid Irish patriot and the British "competent military authority," we shall tell it.

We believe that in times of peace we should work along the lines of peace to strengthen the nation, and we believe that whatever strengthens and elevates the working class strengthens the nation.

But we also believe that in times of war we should act as in war. We despise, entirely despise and loathe, all the mouthings and mouthers about war who infest Ireland in time of peace, just as we despise and loathe all the cantings about caution and restraint to which the same people treat us in times of war.

Mark well, then, our programme. While the war lasts and Ireland still is a subject nation we shall continue to urge her to fight for her freedom.

We shall continue, in season and out of season, to teach that the "far-flung battle line" of England is weakest at the point nearest its heart; that Ireland is in that position of tactical advantage; that a defeat of England in India, Egypt, the Balkans or Flanders would not be so dangerous to the British Empire as any conflict of armed forces in Ireland; that the time for Ireland's battle is NOW, the place for Ireland's battle is HERE; that a strong man may deal lusty blows with his fists against a host of surrounding foes, and conquer, but will succumb if a child sticks a pin in his heart.

But the moment peace is once admitted by the British Government as being a subject ripe for discussion, *that moment our policy will be for peace* and in direct opposition to all talk or preparation for armed revolution.

We will be no party to leading out Irish patriots to meet the might of an England at peace. The moment peace is in the air we shall strictly confine ourselves and lend all our influence to the work of turning the thought of labour in Ireland to the work of peaceful reconstruction.

That is our programme. You can now compare it with the programme of those who bid you hold your hand now, and thus put it in the power of the enemy to patch up a temporary peace, turn round and smash you at his leisure, and then go to war again with the Irish question settled—in the graves of Irish patriots.

We fear that is what is going to happen. It is to our mind inconceivable that the British public should allow conscription to be applied to England and not to Ireland. Nor does the British Government desire it. But that Government will use the cry of the necessities of war to force conscription upon the people of England, and will then make a temporary peace, and turn round to force Ireland to accept the same terms as have been forced upon England.

The English public will gladly see this done—misfortune likes company. The situation will then shape itself thus: The Irish Volunteers who are pledged to fight conscription will either need to swallow their pledge, and see the young men of Ireland conscripted, or will need to resent conscription, and engage the military force of England at a time when England is at peace.

This is what the diplomacy of England is working for, what the stupidity of some of our leaders . . . is making possible. It is our duty, it is the duty of all who wish to save Ireland from such shame or such slaughter, to strengthen the hand of those of the leaders who are for action as against those who are playing into the hands of the enemy.

We are neither rash nor cowardly. We know our opportunity when we see it, and we know when it has gone. We know that at the end of this war England will have an army of at least one million men, or *more than two soldiers for every adult male in Ireland,* and these soldiers veterans of the greatest war in history.

We shall not want to fight those men. We shall devote our attention to organizing their comrades who return to civil life, to organizing them into Trade Unions and Labour Parties to secure them their rights in civil life—unless we emigrate to some country where there are men.

# leon trotsky

Leon Trotsky, a Russian revolutionist, an able theoretician of Marxism, an outstanding writer and orator, and the chief organizer of the primitive Red Army, was the offspring of Jewish parents who lived at Yanovka in the Ukraine; Trotsky's original name was Lev Davidovich Bronstein. His father, a prosperous farmer, sent him to Odessa in 1897 to study mathematics at the New Russia University. He left school the following year, however, and his populist inclinations led him into the Social Democratic (Marxist) circle in Odessa. Arrested for political activities in 1898 and banished to Siberia in 1900, he escaped in 1902, using a forged passport under the name of Trotsky, who was the head jailer of the Odessa prison in which he had been held.

After escaping from Russia, Trotsky traveled to London where he collaborated with Lenin on the revolutionary journal *Iskra* ("Spark"). Intimate contact with Lenin convinced him that Lenin's policies and methods would eventually result in a one-man dictatorship. When the Russian Social Democratic Labor Party split at its second congress in 1903, Trotsky emerged as a leading Menshevik and a forthright opponent of Lenin. It was in Munich during 1904-05 that Trotsky worked out his theory of "Permanent revolution," with the assistance of the Marxist A. I. (Parvus) Helfand. Returning to Russia at the time of the 1905 Revolution, he became chairman of the short-lived St. Petersburg soviet. Arrested and banished again to Siberia in 1907, Trotsky escaped en route, fled abroad once more, and settled in Vienna.

During his years in Vienna, Trotsky edited the pro-Menshevik newspaper *Pravda;* but he also made strenuous efforts to reconcile feuding Menshevik and Bolshevik factions within the Social Democratic movement. The attempt failed when Bolshevik leaders, and some Mensheviks, boycotted his 1912 "August Conference" in Vienna. At the outbreak of the First World War, Trotsky went to Switzerland and then to Paris, where he was active in pacifist and radical propaganda. On the war issue he assumed an "internationalist" position, though he opposed Lenin's advocacy of a defeat for Russia. In 1916 he was deported from France and moved to New York City where he edited, with Bukharin and Kollantai, the paper *Novy Mir* ("New World").

Trotsky returned to Russia in May 1917 following the overthrow of Czar Nicholas II. Upon his arrival in Petrograd (now Leningrad), he joined Lenin and took part in the unsuccessful Bolshevik uprising of July 1917. Trotsky was imprisoned by the Kerensky government, but was released in September and became one of the chief organizers of the October Revolution which brought the Bolsheviks to power.

As people's commissar for foreign affairs, Trotsky led the new Soviet Government's delegation which negotiated the humiliating peace of Brest-Litovsk with Germany. After March 1918, Trotsky was people's commissar for military and naval affairs. He devoted much of his energy to building up the Red Army, and its victory in the subsequent Civil War was in large measure due to him.

Intolerant, tactless, and never one to suffer fools, Trotsky made numerous enemies during the Civil War, most particularly the jealous and vengeful Stalin. After Lenin's death in 1924 Trotsky appeared as the obvious candidate for the leadership, but an alliance between Zinoviev, Kamenev (Trotsky's brother-in-law), and Stalin prevented him from succeeding to power. Although he remained a member of the party's Politburo, he lost his posts in government. Thereafter, until his final defeat in 1927, he was engaged in a continual struggle with his rivals on both political and personal grounds. Advocating world revolution, Trotsky came into increasing conflict with Stalin's plans for "socialism in one country." Trotsky had great prestige as a revolutionary leader and had followers in both the army and the government, but Stalin controlled the party machine. Zinoviev and Kamenev belatedly joined forces with Trotsky in 1926 in an effort to check Stalin's power.

Trotsky was expelled from the Politburo in 1926 and from the Communist Party in 1927. In the following January he was exiled to Siberia and then, in 1929, was ordered to leave the U.S.S.R. entirely. Refused admission by most countries, he was granted asylum by Turkey, where he lived on the Princes'

Islands near Istanbul. Deprived of his Soviet citizenship in 1932, Trotsky lived as
an exile in Turkey (until 1933), France (1933-35), Norway (1935-36), and
finally Mexico (from 1937). He continually denounced Stalin and acted as the
theoretical leader of Trotskyites among foreign Communists. During the public
treason trials held in Moscow during 1936-38, Trotsky was charged with heading
a plot against the Stalinist regime. The accusations, which Trotsky bitterly
denied, cloaked Stalin's real purpose of purging the party ranks of all who might
prove disloyal to him. An international commission under the chairmanship of
the U.S. philosopher John Dewey, set up to inquire into these allegations, rejected them in its report *Not Guilty* (1937). On August 20, 1940, Trotsky was
mortally wounded by a Stalinist agent who had infiltrated the group of followers
that met at Trotsky's home in the suburbs of Mexico City. He died on the
following day.

   Trotsky's prolific writings are reflective of his superlative intelligence—a fact
unchallenged even by his enemies—his indomitable aggressiveness, and his incisive and polemical style. Together with his brilliant political works, Trotsky
wrote on military theory and on problems of cultural life. He was more of a
Marxian purist than most Bolsheviks and he insisted that the Communist Party
should establish a completely classless society in which neither the proletarian
nor any other class was accorded special consideration. He argued in his 1921
book *The Defense of Terrorism* (excerpts from the English edition *Terrorism
and Communism* follow) that the revolutionary class must attain its end by all
methods at its disposal—if necessary, by terrorism. He bitterly condemned
Marxist Karl Kautsky for his objections to terror, brutality, and violence as
appropriate means of consolidating the revolution. Trotsky lived by the creed of
violence and, in 1940, he died by it.

## Terrorism and Communism

... The scheme of the political situation on a world scale is quite clear. The
bourgeoisie, which has brought the nations, exhausted and bleeding to death, to
the brink of destruction—particularly the victorious bourgeoisie—has displayed
its complete inability to bring them out of their terrible situation, and, thereby,
its incompatibility with the future development of humanity. All the inter-
mediate political groups, including here first and foremost the social-patriotic

From Leon Trotsky, *Terrorism and Communism,* The University of Michigan Press, Ann
Arbor, Michigan, 1961, pp. 35-41, 54-55, 57-59.

parties, are rotting alive. The proletariat they have deceived is turning against them more and more every day, and is becoming strengthened in its revolutionary convictions as the only power that can save the peoples from savagery and destruction. However, history has not at all secured, just at this moment, a formal parliamentary majority on the side of the party of the social revolution. In other words, history has not transformed the nation into a debating society solemnly voting the transition to the social revolution by a majority of votes. On the contrary, the violent revolution has become a necessity precisely because the imminent requirements of history are helpless to find a road through the apparatus of parliamentary democracy. The capitalist bourgeois calculates: "while I have in my hands lands, factories, workshops, banks; while I possess newspapers, universities, schools; while—and this most important of all—I retain control of the army; the apparatus of democracy, however you reconstruct it, will remain obedient to my will. I subordinate to my interests spiritually the stupid, conservative, characterless lower middle class, just as it is subjected to me materially. I oppress, and will oppress, its imagination by the gigantic scale of my buildings, my transactions, my plans, and my crimes. For moments when it is dissatisfied and murmurs, I have created scores of safety-valves and lightning-conductors. At the right moment I will bring into existence opposition parties, which will disappear tomorrow, but which to-day accomplish their mission by affording the possibility of the lower middle class expressing their indignation without hurt therefrom for capitalism. I shall hold the masses of the people, under cover of compulsory general education, on the verge of complete ignorance, giving them no opportunity of rising above the level which my experts in spiritual slavery consider safe. I will corrupt, deceive, and terrorize the more privileged or the more backward of the proletariat itself. By means of these measures, I shall not allow the vanguard of the working class to gain the ear of the majority of the working class, while the necessary weapons of mastery and terrorism remain in my hands."

To this the revolutionary proletarian replies: "Consequently, the first condition of salvation is to tear the weapons of domination out of the hands of the bourgeoisie. It is hopeless to think of a peaceful arrival to power while the bourgeoisie retains in its hands all the apparatus of power. Three times over hopeless is the idea of coming to power by the path which the bourgeoisie itself indicates and, at the same time, barricades—the path of parliamentary democracy. There is only one way: to seize power, taking away from the bourgeoisie the material apparatus of government. Independently of the superficial balance of forces in parliament, I shall take over for social administration the chief forces and resources of production. I shall free the mind of the lower middle class from their capitalist hypnosis. I shall show them in practice what is the meaning of

Socialist production. Then even the most backward, the most ignorant, or most terrorized sections of the nation will support me, and willingly and intelligently will join in the work of social construction."

When the Russian Soviet Government dissolved the Constituent Assembly, that fact seemed to the leading Social-Democrats of Western Europe, if not the beginning of the end of the world, at all events a rude and arbitrary break with all the previous developments of Socialism. In reality, it was only the inevitable outcome of the new position resulting from imperialism and the war. If Russian Communism was the first to enter the path of casting up theoretical and practical accounts, this was due to the same historical reasons which forced the Russian proletariat to be the first to enter the path of the struggle for power.

All that has happened since then in Europe bears witness to the fact that we drew the right conclusions. To imagine that democracy can be restored in its general purity means that one is living in a pitiful, reactionary utopia.

... The doctrine of formal democracy is not scientific Socialism, but the theory of so-called natural law.

... If we look back to the historical sequence of world concepts, the theory of natural law will prove to be a paraphrase of Christian spiritualism freed from its crude mysticism. The Gospels proclaimed to the slave, that he had just the same soul as the slave-owner, and in this way established the equality of all men before the heavenly tribunal. In reality, the slave remained a slave, and obedience became for him a religious duty. In the teaching of Christianity, the slave found an expression for his own ignorant protest against his degraded condition. Side by side with the protest was also the consolation. Christianity told him:— "You have an immortal soul, although you resemble a pack-horse." Here sounded the note of indignation. But the same Christianity said:—"Although you are like a pack-horse, yet your immortal soul has in store for it an eternal reward." Here is the voice of consolation. These two notes were found in historical Christianity in different proportions at different periods and amongst different classes. But, as a whole, Christianity, like all other religions, became a method of deadening the consciousness of the oppressed masses.

Natural law, which developed into the theory of democracy, said to the worker: "all men are equal before the law, independently of their origin, their property, and their position; every man has an equal right in determining the fate of the people." This ideal criterion revolutionized the consciousness of the masses in so far as it was a condemnation of absolutism, aristocratic privileges, and the property qualification. But the longer it went on, the more it sent the consciousness to sleep, legalizing poverty, slavery and degradation: for how could one revolt against slavery when every man has an equal right in determining the fate of the nation?

. . . In the practical interests of the development of the working class, the Socialist Party took its stand at a certain period on the path of parliamentarism. But this did not mean in the slightest that it accepted in principle the meta-physical theory of democracy, based on extra-historical, super-class rights. The proletarian doctrines examined democracy as the instrument of bourgeois society entirely adapted to the problems and requirements of the ruling classes; but as bourgeois society lived by the labor of the proletariat and could not deny it the legalization of a certain part of its class struggle without destroying itself, this gave the Socialist Party the possibility of utilizing, at a certain period, and within certain limits, the mechanism of democracy, without taking an oath to do so as an unshakable principle.

The root problem of the party, at all periods of its struggle, was to create the conditions for real, economic, living equality for mankind as members of a united human commonwealth. It was just for this reason that the theoreticians of the proletariat had to expose the metaphysics of democracy as a philosophic mask for political mystification.

The democratic party at the period of its revolutionary enthusiasm, when exposing the enslaving and stupefying lie of church dogma, preached to the masses:—"You are lulled to sleep by promises of eternal bliss at the end of your life, while here you have no rights and you are bound with the chains of tyranny." The Socialist Party, a few decades later, said to the same masses with no less right:—"You are lulled to sleep with the fiction of civic equality and political rights, but you are deprived of the possibility of realizing those rights. Conditional and shadowy legal equality has been transformed into the convicts' chain with which each of you is fastened to the chariot of capitalism."

In the name of its fundamental task, the Socialist Party mobilized the masses on the parliamentary ground as well as on others; but nowhere and at no time did any party bind itself to bring the masses to Socialism only through the gates of democracy. In adapting ourselves to the parliamentary regime, we stopped at a theoretical exposure of democracy, because we were still too weak to over-come it in practice. But the path of Socialist ideas which is visible through all deviations, and even betrayals, foreshadows no other outcome but this: to throw democracy aside and replace it by the mechanism of the proletariat, at the moment when the latter is strong enough to carry out such a task.

. . . The problem of revolution, as of war, consists in breaking the will of the foe, forcing him to capitulate and to accept the conditions of the conqueror. The will, of course, is a fact of the physical world, but in contradistinction to a meeting, a dispute, or a congress, the revolution carries out its object by means of the employment of material resources—though to a less degree than war. The bourgeoisie itself conquered power by means of revolts, and consolidated it by the civil war. In the peaceful period, it retains power by means of a system of repression. As long as class society, founded on the most deep-rooted antagonisms, continues to exist, repression remains a necessary means of breaking the will of the opposing side.

Even if, in one country or another, the dictatorship of the proletariat grew up within the external framework of democracy, this would by no means avert the civil war. The question as to who is to rule the country, i.e., of the life or death of the bourgeoisie, will be decided on either side, not by references to the paragraphs of the constitution, but by the employment of all forms of violence.

... The degree of ferocity of the struggle depends on a series of internal and international circumstances. The more ferocious and dangerous is the resistance of the class enemy who have been overthrown, the more inevitably does the system of repression take the form of a system of terror.

... The Russian proletariat was the first to enter the path of the social revolution, and the Russian bourgeoisie, politically helpless, was emboldened to struggle against its political and economic expropriation only because it saw its elder sister in all countries still in power, and still maintaining economic, political, and, to a certain extent, military supremacy.

If our November revolution had taken place a few months, or even a few weeks, after the establishment of the rule of the proletariat in Germany, France, and England, there can be no doubt that our revolution would have been the most "peaceful," the most "bloodless" of all possible revolutions on this sinful earth. But this historical sequence—the most "natural" at the first glance, and, in any case, the most beneficial for the Russian working class—found itself infringed—not through our fault, but through the will of events. Instead of being the last, the Russian proletariat proved to be the first. It was just this circumstance, after the first period of confusion, that imparted desperation to the character of the resistance of the classes which had ruled in Russia previously, and forced the Russian proletariat, in a moment of the greatest peril, foreign attacks, and internal plots and insurrections, to have recourse to severe measures of State terror. No one will now say that those measures proved futile. But, perhaps, we are expected to consider them "intolerable"?

The working class, which seized power in battle, had as its object and its duty to establish that power unshakeably, to guarantee its own supremacy beyond question, to destroy its enemies' hankering for a new revolution, and thereby to make sure of carrying out Socialist reforms. Otherwise there would be no point in seizing power.

The revolution "logically" does not demand terrorism, just as "logically" it does not demand an armed insurrection. What a profound commonplace! But the revolution does require of the revolutionary class that it should attain its end by all methods at its disposal—if necessary, to an armed rising: if required, by terrorism. A revolutionary class which has conquered power with arms in its hands is bound to, and will, suppress, rifle in hand, all attempts to tear the power out of its hands. Where it has against it a hostile army, it will oppose to it its own army. Where it is confronted with armed conspiracy, attempt at murder, or rising, it will hurl at the heads of its enemies an unsparing penalty. Perhaps Kautsky has invented other methods? Or does he reduce the whole question to the *degree* of repression, and recommend in all circumstances imprisonment instead of execution?

The question of the form of repression, or of its degree, of course, is not one of "principle." It is a question of expediency. In a revolutionary period, the party, which has been thrown from power, which does not reconcile itself with the stability of the ruling class, and which proves this by its desperate struggle against the latter, cannot be terrorized by the threat of imprisonment, as it does not believe in its duration. It is just this simple but decisive fact that explains the widespread recourse to shooting in a civil war.

Or, perhaps, Kautsky wishes to say that execution is not expedient, that "classes cannot be cowed." This is untrue. Terror is helpless—and then only "in the long run"—if it is employed by reaction against a historically rising class. But terror can be very efficient against a reactionary class which does not want to leave the scene of operations. *Intimidation* is a powerful weapon of policy, both internationally and internally. War like revolution, is founded upon intimidation. A victorious war, generally speaking, destroys only an insignificant part of the conquered army, intimidating the remainder and breaking their will. The revolution works in the same way: it kills individuals, and intimidates thousands. In this sense, the Red Terror is not distinguishable from the armed insurrection, the direct continuation of which it represents. The State terror of a revolutionary class can be condemned "morally" only by a man who, as a principle, rejects (in words) every form of violence whatsoever—consequently, every war and every rising. For this one has to be merely and simply a hypocritical Quaker.

"But, in that case, in what do your tactics differ from the tactics of Tsarism?" we are asked, by the high priests of Liberalism and Kautskianism.

You do not understand this, holy men? We shall explain to you. The terror of Tsarism was directed against the proletariat. The gendarmerie of Tsarism throttled the workers who were fighting for the Socialist order. Our Extraordinary Commissions shoot landlords, capitalists, and generals who are striving to restore the capitalist order. Do you grasp this . . . distinction? Yes? For us Communists it is quite sufficient.